1948

U.S. Water Pollution Control Act passed

1962

Esalen Institute, an alternative educational center in Big Sur, CA, founded

1969

U.S. National Environmental Policy Act passed and Environmental Protection Agency created

1968

First issue of Stewart Brand's *Whole Earth Catalog* published

1954

Scott and Helen Nearing's *Living the Good Life* published

1967

Environmental Defense Fund founded

1969

Union Oil Co. oil disaster off Santa Barbara, CA

1962

Rachel Carson's *Silent Spring* published

1969

Don't Make a Wave Committee established

1949

Aldo Leopold's *Sand County Almanac* published

HANDMADE HOUSES

HANDMADE HOUSES

A Century of Earth-Friendly Home Design

RICHARD OLSEN

New York · Paris · London · Milan

Prince Karim Aga Khan IV responds to reporters while standing beneath a framework of twisted juniper—part of a Sardinian peasant-style structure for his ecological resort the Costa Smeralda. Sardinia, Italy, 1960s.

CONTENTS

PREFACE

IN MAY OF 2003, while living in New York City and working as the architecture and design editor for a book publisher, I received an unexpected gift from the wife of one of my authors: first-edition copies of 1974's *Woodstock Handmade Houses*, by Robert Haney, David Ballantine, and Jonathan Elliott; and *Craftsmen of Necessity*, by Christopher and Charlotte Williams— books that came out when I was five years old. "To Richard. 5-11-03," Carolyn Johnson Morgan wrote on the title page of *Woodstock*. "It is interesting to think that 30 years have passed since these books (and the movement they represent) appeared. Strange, too, to see the children of the Flower Children driving SUVs and living in McMansions."

It was via "handcraft" that I'd landed in architecture and design publishing. My great-grandfather, Trygve Olsen, was a carpenter and builder of houses. After he left Norway and emigrated to the United States, ending up in New York, he passed along to my grandfather, Bjarne Olsen, those same old-world skills together with many of his wonderful nineteenth-century hand tools. Some of my earliest childhood memories are of me stand-

OPPOSITE: Big Sur outlaw builder Bob Nash in Sedona, Arizona, 1974, channeling light energy with one of his stained-glass pieces. Nash's work, especially his ceramic tiles, appears in some of Big Sur's most iconic handmade houses. BELOW AND FOLLOWING PAGES: Required reading from the handmade house library.

ing on a stool in front of my grandfather's 1900s maple workbench, watching him meticulously join two pieces of wood or doing my best to chisel or hammer whatever I could get my hands on. Later, I was the kid in the neighborhood building wood go-karts and skateboards, scrounging for lumber to construct large-scale half-pipes and other skateboard ramps. As an adult, when I was renovating my Brooklyn apartment, I took the leftover wood from the 20' x 20' sliding-ladder bookshelf that I'd built into a wall and made side tables, an entertainment center, and a bed—furniture I still use and feel mostly good about. I don't know that I possess the carpentry talents of my great-grandfather or grandfather—probably not—but working with wood always feels right.

For at least a moment, Morgan's gift took me out of the strictly governed worlds of "architecture and design," endeavors that, in books especially, tend to be treated as separate from the handcrafts of carpentry and construction. It took me back to the simple pleasure of *building*, an experience I'd (somehow) filed away in my childhood memories. In *Woodstock Handmade Houses* I found a new world, what the late historian Henry Elder called "the architecture of protest." It was the woodbutcher design and construction—exuberant, sensual, one-of-a-kind owner-built structures made largely from salvage and mostly outside of building codes. In the Williams' book, I was reminded that simplicity, whether in a building or

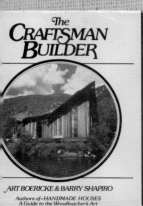

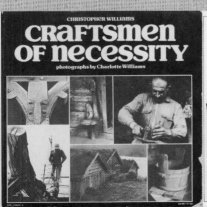

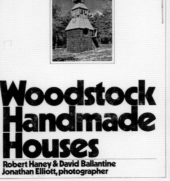

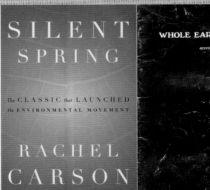

object, is always worth pursuing and often yields the most complex results. Morgan had inscribed that *Craftsmen of Necessity* is like a bible to her. I could see why.

In 2006, after authoring *Log Houses of the World*, a book on the last two centuries of log-house design and construction, I took the job of architecture editor at *Architectural Digest* in Los Angeles. Almost five years later, I had participated in the publication of dozens of articles on award-winning houses and enjoyed the kind of access to famous architects and world-class architecture that only *that* magazine can bring. Throughout this period, though, the comparatively modest handmade house was fixed in my imagination. The more time I spent looking for them in places like Big Sur, Marin County, Topanga Canyon, and even in Malibu, the more I was convinced that it was time to revisit this subject in a big way. There was much more to this subject, more to the art and craft and social consciousness of it, than was depicted in the Woodstock book.

True handmade houses possess a certain feeling that's unlike anything I've experienced in a building. They're imbued with love. As soon as you sit down in front of the fireplace, as soon as you observe the connection their owners have with them, you get it. But there's also a very practical side to their appeal. As the cultural focus on environmental issues has again intensified (as

industry has raced to cash in on all the new interest in "green" with more technological products), it seemed that it would almost be irresponsible not to revisit the made-from-salvage handmade house, the kind of design and construction that Canadian architect and master builder Henry Yorke Mann calls "common-sense green."

It's true that you can't build this way everywhere, and maybe you shouldn't be able to. But still, today no other approach to home design seems as valid.

* * *

This book is partly intended as a journey through the evolution of the handmade house over the last century. It aims to provide the kind of historical backdrop that can lead to a full appreciation of the subject and an understanding of where it could go. With much of the development of handmade houses occurring in the 1960s and '70s, it's not without color.

The introduction identifies the "hot spots" of the handmade house's roots and growth, the places where the socioeconomic conditions were conducive to building and living this way. It looks at some of the individuals and works that gave each place its rich character. It considers how this design language developed, not only in the United States but also in Canada, the United Kingdom, Europe, and in Australia. It also points out how, in the 1980s and '90s, the handmade house's id-

iosyncratic salvage aesthetic was transported out of the country and made into an urban design style, one that's since become very much a part of the identities of popular decorators and large corporate retailers like Ralph Lauren, Restoration Hardware, and Anthropologie.

The Origins section calls out some of the primary sources of inspiration for the architects, artists, carpenters, and other craftspeople featured in the book. These individuals and buildings paved the way.

The heart of this book is divided into two parts, "Architecture without Architects" and "Architecture with Architects," a respectful nod to the late Bernard Rudofsky's widely influential survey from 1964, *Architecture without Architects: A Short Introduction to Non-Pedigreed Architecture*. The "owner-built" examples are showcased separately from the architects' "design-build" examples. (Although they're very much related in terms of aesthetics, the two camps take different routes to the end result.) The individuals and the houses chosen to represent the two groups collectively show the possibilities of the handmade house of the last century. These are some of the greatest handmade houses ever built.

In these two sections, the coverage begins in the 1950s and extends to the late 2000s. One of these houses was made with only $1,000. Others were made with not much more than that. Some of them made their first public debut nearly 40 years ago in books such as *Handmade Houses: A Guide to the Woodbutcher's Art*, by Art Boericke and Barry Shapiro; *Shelter*, by Lloyd Kahn; and the other 1970s books that first popularized this subject. I wanted to learn how those dwellings have held up over the years, not just structurally but also ideologically, and to see if and how they've accommodated their original owners' changing needs. The results of those investigations are all here.

For each of the 23 houses in these two sections, new photography provides an up-close portrait, while the text strives to paint a picture of the passionate people and often-trying circumstances behind the scenes. Finally, all of these talented and daring builders and their unforgettable houses are gathered in one place. Their stories are fascinating, and their homes may prompt you to rethink your own.

A NOTE ON EARTHSHIPS

While the underlying philosophy of the Earthship buildings in Taos, New Mexico, has much to do with these mostly timber-and-stone handmade houses, the materials employed by the Earthships—automobile tires, beer cans, and bottles, refrigerator panels, and other pieces of the garbage-dump population—adds a significant degree of aesthetic separation. They're their own compelling story, their own book.

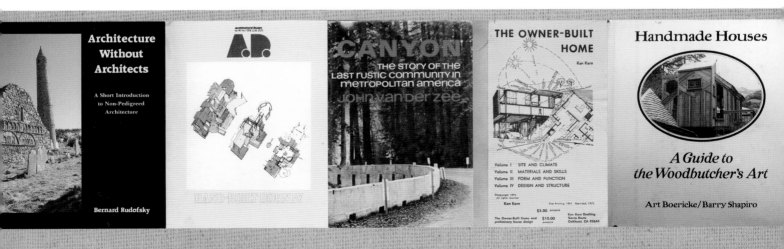

INTRODUCTION: *Mapping a Movement*

"*Most men appear never to have considered what a house is, and are actually though needlessly poor all their lives because they think they must have such a one as their neighbors have.*"

—HENRY DAVID THOREAU, *WALDEN*, 1854

"*Hundreds of textbooks have been written, covering every period of domestic architecture, interior ornamentation and furnishing, from oldest Egyptian antiquities to latest modern obliquities. But the personality of a house, the quality that appeals not merely to our critical faculties but to our personal emotions, has been left out altogether—overlooked perhaps, or possibly taken for granted, as though a collection of valuable possessions must of themselves confer charm. And yet charm is precisely what the majority of houses lack. We pass all sorts of adequately designed and neatly cared-for houses, much as we pass all sorts of neatly presentable and might-be-agreeable people on the street, without noticing them at all.*"

—EMILY POST, *THE PERSONALITY OF A HOUSE: THE BLUE BOOK OF HOME CHARM*, 1930

TAKE A MOMENT TO STEP INSIDE a house in which cost-cutting DIY ingenuity and improvisation, eco-sensitivity, and craft coexist. The building has little in common with what you've seen in the shelter magazines. Many of its materials are "rescues." Instead of being hidden behind Sheetrock, the construction of those parts emphasizes honesty—the wood, the stone, the other natural materials left undressed and breathable on the interior and exterior. The detailing was done by hand, and by being a celebration of the human touch, in protest of machine-made predictability,

OPPOSITE: On Cavallo Island, France, in the villa of Vittorio Emanuele di Savoia, Prince of Naples, a stair was carved from one of the site's existing granite boulders, the work of architect Savin Couëlle.

it's deliberately imperfect. The rooms are unusually layered, with rich and varied textures. Overall, there's an unmistakable feeling of warmth and a sense of history, perhaps even a feeling of primitiveness—no matter how old the house may in fact be. This is the "handmade house." It's low-tech, if not anti-tech. It's "slow" architecture. It comes more from the solar plexus than from the head. You can't build this kind of dwelling with the uniform materials available at your local big-box home-improvement store.

Many of the most thrilling handmade houses were realized in the 1960s and '70s, during the height of the counterculture and back-to-the-land movements that took place in the United States and beyond. These were anything but settled times. In just the States, there was free speech and Vietnam War protesting and

In handmade houses, great artistic emphasis is often placed on doors, especially front doors, which many regard as the house's handshake. Nowhere is this exemplified more beautifully than at James Hubbell's Boys' House in San Diego County, California.

rioting; the assassinations of John F. Kennedy, Robert F. Kennedy, and Martin Luther King, Jr.; the civil rights movement; rampant crime and decay in the nation's urban centers; the environmental crisis; and the oil crisis. In response, increasing numbers of individuals were fleeing the cities, settling in the country (at that time you could still find desirable cheap land), and building what people were calling a handmade house. It was one way of taking control of your life. This kind of architecture was, itself, a protest.

For the builders, many of whom were college-educated 20-somethings making for themselves or for struggling-artist friends, what was considered new and contemporary and representative of the latest technology wasn't serving the culture. Primitive ways, the blatantly rustic, hand-oriented ways of old, appeared more valid and meaningful. However, while they shared an outlook, these individuals weren't all part of the same constituency. Some were design-build architects; some were artist-carpenters; some were simply do-it-yourself types.

As information and enthusiasm about this kind of building spread, the designs started sharing certain characteristics. The look was becoming codified. By 1973, when Lloyd Kahn's *Shelter* and Art Boericke and Barry Shapiro's *Handmade Houses: A Guide to the Woodbutcher's Art* landed in bookstores across the United States, each unveiling a wide range of examples, it was finally possible for anyone to see the handmade house for what it had become: a movement of its own. Throughout the '70s, this approach, whether it was called "owner-built" or "woodbutcher style" or "handmade," would continue to thrive and evolve and find new adherents. It was in tune with the tenor of the times.

The Reagan era, 1981 to 1989, changed the course. Just as they were to other symbols of environmental consciousness and nonconformity, the years of Ronald Reagan's presidency were largely inhospitable to this way of building and living. Ironically, it was the aggressive conservatism of Reagan's two-term California governorship, from 1967 to '75, that had to a great degree sparked the architectural and lifestyle protests that the handmade house came to symbolize.

After the tragedies of September 11, 2001, the tides changed again. On the streets of New York, Washington, DC, Chicago, Dallas, San Francisco, Los Angeles and other major cities across the country, a feeling of disenchantment, distrust, and vulnerability pervaded.

As had taken place during the 1970s back-to-the-land movement, many of those who could afford to relocate got out and retreated to a rural life. Others with the necessary means went to the country to create secondary residences—a "just-in-case" measure. A new back-to-the-land movement was underway, this time led by members of Generation X. Once again, designing and building a house for one's self, a symbol of self-sufficiency, a path to deeper meaning and connection in what had all the signs of a troubled world, felt right.

In an effort to cut costs or be environmentally responsible or both, or simply because they like the aged look, many individuals of the twenty-first-century back-to-the-land movement turned to salvaged materials. In fast-increasing numbers, as had happened three decades earlier, old barns were being dismantled and trucked off to new building sites.

In the last decade, our ever-deepening dependency on the laptop, the tablet, the smartphone, and the e-reader has led to a less-than-surprising backlash: a sweeping revival of making things with our own hands. It, too, is not unlike the one that reached coast to coast in the '70s, when in the suburbs it was common to see neighbors going door to door selling macrame plant hangers and other crafty wares. In fact, much of contemporary crafting's growth explosion is owed to the networking possibilities of the Internet. You don't have to go door to door anymore. It's the same conflicted convenience factor that's made it easy to ignore what's available right in your own neighborhood and, in a matter of a few carbon footprint–expanding mouse clicks, get Queen Anne windows from England, Baroque doors from France, and Art Nouveau tile from Spain shipped to the site of your new handmade house.

In 2006, Al Gore's Oscar-winning documentary, *An Inconvenient Truth*, brought worldwide attention to global warming and ozone-layer depletion and, just as Rachel Carson's book *Silent Spring* did in the 1960s, made environmental consciousness popular. It's the same kind of enthusiasm that had played such a big part in the handmade house's 1970s popularity. That wave continues to build.

More recently, the 2008 economic crash and our ongoing recovery from it has many of us contemplating the benefits of the "reduce, reuse, recycle" principle as it applies to our homes. Many of us still want our living spaces to speak for us to some degree, but now we have to accomplish that in ways more creative and responsible. The handmade house, or at least certain defining aspects of it, ought to be a part of this thinking, now and in the future, no matter if you're living in the city or the country.

In tracing the development of the aesthetic that was first popularized in books such as 1973's *Handmade Houses: A Guide to the Woodbutcher's Art*, what's since become a design style, the starting point is California. There, the early epicenters were Marin County, the tiny East Bay community of Canyon, and Big Sur. Parts of British Columbia, Canada, including Vancouver and the Gulf Islands, also played a defining formative role. On the East Coast, the greatest contributions came out of a small community in Vermont called Prickly Mountain. In between the coasts, there were important strides made, too, and the phenomenon didn't belong exclusively to North America. The spirit, energy, and values systems that are behind the making of these houses also exist in parts of the United Kingdom, Europe, and Australia. The images presented in this section offer glances in each of these locations.

Big Sur, California

ABOVE: In talks about their iconic handmade houses, Big Sur's old-guard builders seldom overlook the storybook Cement House, the former home of *Indians in Overalls* author Jaime de Angulo. Designed by de Angulo and built in 1933 with help from Al and George Foster, Sam Trotter, and Ed Melville, the charm is behind that Dutch door: walk-in sculpted-cement Gothic fireplaces in every room, hand-split redwood framing, and redwood pole columns. The celebrated photographer Wynn Bullock often used the house's interior in his work.

OPPOSITE, BOTTOM: The 1933 Overstrom House was a single-wall redwood structure with redwood cabinets and a redwood-block floor, all designed and lovingly crafted with hand tools by Swedish immigrant carpenter Gustave Overstrom, with help from Sam Trotter. Situated a five-mile hike (or mule ride) up a steep ridge near Partington Creek, the house couldn't be saved in the 2008 Basin Complex fire. In 1971, before historian Jeff Norman moved in, a houseguest enjoys a cup of tea in the classic Big Sur kitchen. ABOVE: House designed by Walter Trotter and built in 1950 (before electricity) on Pfeiffer Ridge for artist Emile Norman and his partner, Brooks Clement, photographed a few years after it was built. LEFT: The influential late 1920s house of Big Sur pioneer Alexandrine Boronda is sheathed in redwood barn shakes.

ABOVE, LEFT: The unattributed Waterfall
House (left) is one of the pioneer buildings
that the Esalen Institute inherited upon its
founding in 1962. The original all-redwood
structure had a shake roof, rough board
siding, and reclaimed small-pane windows.
After '64, the inaugural year of Esalen's
popular annual folk-music festival, the
Waterfall House, along with Esalen buildings such as the Fritz Perls House by Selig
Morgenrath, would become a point of reference for back-to-the-land builders. ABOVE,
RIGHT: Architect George Brook-Kothlow and his
painter/potter wife, Jennifer Brook-Kothlow,
sit on a stack of reclaimed redwood bridge
timbers, the building material for his
latest project, 1966's Hill of the Hawk.
LEFT: In 1967, also on Esalen's property,
jewelry designer Goph Albitz was mining
the possibilities of outsider architecture
for himself, drawing inspiration from the
Waterfall House. OPPOSITE, TOP: The seminal
Hill of the Hawk, a high-art handmade house
in the mode of Mark Mills's nearby "Wild
Bird" for Nathaniel and Margaret Owings,
teamed Brook-Kothlow with builder Lloyd
Kahn. Later, before joining Stewart Brand
in the *Whole Earth Catalog*, Kahn would
build his own handmade house in Big Sur.

BOTTOM LEFT: In 1969, when the *Los Angeles Times Home* magazine published the house, they described how reclaimed timber had been used for the structure, the siding, and the floor, emphasizing, "None of these is finished or treated in any way." The living room of Hill of the Hawk, 41 years after that influential publication. BOTTOM RIGHT: Built on the Anderson Creek site where convict laborers were housed during the making of the highway and, later, where painter Jean Varda, sculptor Barbara Spring, and writer Henry Miller each lived at one time, the house of Tony and Marguerite Staude came about as a result of Hill of the Hawk's publication. Staude acquired the necessary redwood bridge timbers for $1,500. Brook-Kothlow's progressive design further elevated the handmade aesthetic.

from the moment he landed. LEFT: Kas and son Gabriel at Mucha Vista in '71. ABOVE: Artist Bob Nash and friends, seated in front of his handmade house and beside his pottery studio and kiln. Nash's shelter was aggressively anti-architecture. In its total rejection of consumer culture, its value as a symbol was immeasurable. RIGHT: In the 1980s, using wood from demolished older houses in the area and glass from an office building in San Francisco, a couple designed and built a cabin over a creek. With its Dutch door and board-and-batten redwood siding, the house is a poetic extension of the local back-to-the-land epoch. "Honoring and learning from the past is a continuous and important effort of love," says one of the owners.

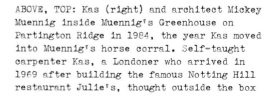

ABOVE, TOP: Kas (right) and architect Mickey Muennig inside Muennig's Greenhouse on Partington Ridge in 1984, the year Kas moved into Muennig's horse corral. Self-taught carpenter Kas, a Londoner who arrived in 1969 after building the famous Notting Hill restaurant Julie's, thought outside the box

Canyon, California

In the 1960s and '70s, Canyon had a disproportionate number of young carpenters, some of whom continue to reside there, such as Barry Smith and Dean Pratt. The leader of the Canyon scene, however, was sculptor and carpenter Deva Rajan. While influenced by the designs and collaborative building practices of Greene & Greene, Bernard Maybeck, and Julia Morgan, Rajan was perhaps most passionate about the design and construction of Fort Ross, an 1812 Russian settlement in Sonoma County. For years, he and his friends had visited the heavy-timber buildings to sketch design details and analyze craftsmanship. In '73, after the fort's chapel burned, Rajan and his company, Canyon Construction, won the restoration commission. Rajan and his team even re-created the methods of construction, relying entirely on hand tools. ABOVE, LEFT: Rajan (in vest) overseeing the sourcing and preparation of the necessary redwood. OPPOSITE, TOP LEFT: An old curved drawknife used often by Rajan and his team. OPPOSITE, BOTTOM LEFT: One of the distinctive doors—source material for the doors at Rajan's own house. OPPOSITE, RIGHT: Splitting the shakes with a froe and a bowling pin.

In 1968, Canyon Construction's family-like crew of artist-carpenters designed and built a 4,750-square-foot handmade house—a $150,000 job—for Michael and Flicka Leibert's 80-acre property in the hills of Pleasanton, California. As was their signature, the crew improvised many of the details on-site. For his materials, Rajan drew from the same San Francisco Hall of Justice fir-timber stock-pile with which he'd started building his own house, combining it with other salvage—barn wood, shipyard cargo booms, rail trestles, and Bay Area Rapid Transit scaffolding. Once the structural timbers and siding was in place, the entire structure, inside and out, was sandblasted for a clean finish, the exterior's blond patina contrasting with an emerald sod roof. TOP LEFT: A number of Canyon women were builders and some worked on the Leibert House. BOTTOM LEFT: Board-wall construction, Canyon style: Battenless 4" x 12" fir diagonal planking, spliced (weather-proofed) beneath the surface with galvanized metal. BOTTOM CENTER: Tay and a friend ride his BMW R69S past the Leibert's in-progress garage/wine-cellar. ABOVE, RIGHT: Rajan on the ladder, fine-tuning. Former Canyon resident Tim Biggins, who worked on the Leibert job, recalls what it was like being a Rajan employee during the project: "One day I was on a roof, and I could tell that Deva had been watching me. After a while, he came up and asked me to take the day off. And I said, 'What's going on?' And he replied, 'I can see you're not having a good time. You're struggling. I don't want that energy going into this building, so I'm going to give you the day off.' So I said to him, 'Geez, you know, I'm pretty tight, with school tuition and whatnot.' And Deva said, 'Oh, I'll pay you. Just take the day off.' That was his way—whatever energy you generate making the building, stays in the building." OPPOSITE, TOP: In 1973–74, using salvaged fir and redwood, carpenter and blacksmith Dean Pratt built his tour de force House I in

the community. Sculptor Bruce Johnson carved some of the beam ends. ABOVE, LEFT: In '69, *Ramparts* magazine documented the community's many building-code-defying handmade houses and their builders' fight to save them from condemnation. "Bob, Sue, and their son Reevan," seated beneath a tree house (built by a 12-year-old local), gave the article certain poignancy—a reminder that this was something that even young families did.

ABOVE, RIGHT: In 1979, the second Pratt-designed-and-constructed house was started, in collaboration with his glassblower/ sculptor/potter/carpenter wife, Louise—it is the couple's current residence. Typical of Pratt's handmade houses, it's an "art as architecture" kind of building, with a 6-inch-thick butcher-block floor and carvings in posts and beams and other personalized woodwork in every room.

Marin County, California

In 1959, 28-year-old architect Daniel Liebermann was commissioned by his parents to design and build two residences (his first) in Mill Valley: a substantial house for them and, on the same 6-acre property, a less-than-1,000-square-foot house that would be for him and his young family. In creating his place, Liebermann arrived at a career-making prototype, an ecologically progressive formula that, in terms of constructional craft and materials, emphasized the hand and played with how far one could take the Japanese concept of *shibui*. (The wood, stone, and metals that he selected each had histories, conveyed by their patinas. The source

was a salvage yard.) Built in 1960, the prototype was the creative breathing room that
the former apprentice to Frank Lloyd Wright
needed to escape "the Wright curse" and move
forward on his own. Following this same
path, he says he's done between 30 and 35
houses, all in California. OPPOSITE, RIGHT:
Liebermann in 2010, beside the treelike
steel column in the living area of the
Inverness house he designed and built in
1997 for himself. OPPOSITE, LEFT: The roof
construction of Liebermann's reclaimed-timber
house includes salvaged-slate fascias,
a fireproofing measure. OPPOSITE, BOTTOM
RIGHT: At Liebermann's c. 1991 McGrath
House in Piedmont, a stair's cascading board
handrail is made with 120-year-old vertical-
grain Douglas fir that came out of St.
Mary's Medical Center in San Francisco.
Rhonda Fleming was the principal artisan

of the finish work. ABOVE: The architect's
prototypical work, the 1960 Liebermann House
in Mill Valley. FOLLOWING PAGE: In the early
1950s, eccentric carpenter and aspiring jazz
musician Roger Somers moved to the Muir Woods
at the southwest flank of Mount Tamalpais
and began a decades' long relationship with
a cluster of circa-1930, mostly redwood farm
buildings. Dubbed "Druid Heights" by one of
his neighbors, poet Elsa Gidlow, this enclave
would evolve into a legendary bohemian way
station and a hub of handcraft-focused,
eco-minded, rogue construction. Somers's
Japanese-organic-meets-Surrealism aesthetic,
which was usually done with plywood and
other low-cost materials, gave the renovated
and new buildings their flamboyant, often
sexually charged distinction. In the fall
of '65, Ed Stiles joined the community,
setting up a woodshop for the crafting of his

organic-Modern furniture designs and sculpture and eventually acquiring one of the farm buildings, an all-redwood converted chicken barn. That structure, too, would end up repeatedly modified, always with the kind of handwork that Stiles brought to his furniture for clients like Graham Nash of Crosby, Stills & Nash. Somers and Stiles had roles in the construction of the Trident, the famous Sausalito restaurant and rock-star hangout. In '69, around the same time that Somers was working on the Mushroom House (TOP) in Bolinas with architect Reese Clark, Stiles, with help from Somers, added to Druid Heights a building he called Mandala (BOTTOM). The salvaged-redwood cabin was the brief and final residence of Zen Buddhism scholar Alan Watts. Later, Mandala served as Somers's home, and in 2001 the carpenter died there while soaking in its hot tub. Stiles, who was also one of the pioneers of the 1970s redwood hot-tub phenomenon, continues to live in the chicken barn and now runs a company that builds houses with architectural salvage. OPPOSITE, LEFT: In the fall of 1971, the University of California, Berkeley's College of Environmental Design offered a field course on designing and building handmade houses. Created and instructed by Jim Campe and Sim Van der Ryn and held on Van der Ryn's Inverness land, the course Making a Place in the Country proved a big success. By the next semester, the students had published a passionate chronicle of their experiences. "We live partly in a physical world and partly in our image of it," wrote student Rob Strauss in its pages. "Making a place in the country forces a physical world on us and demands some new images of us. Some old images get flushed into the open and we can look at them. This publication helped us see the process." OPPOSITE, TOP RIGHT: One of the buildings made by the UC Berkeley class, the Ark, still stands on Van der Ryn's property. In fact, it looks better than ever. Recently, the house was thoroughly renovated by David Hastings, a retired research chemist turned carpenter-builder. Hastings lives there with his partner, Sara Morris, an artist and minority-student advocate. OPPOSITE, BOTTOM RIGHT: The Ark's living room, with interior decoration by Sara Morris. The oil paintings are by Wendy Schwartz.

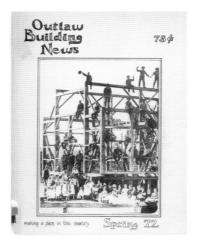

Malibu, California

THIS PAGE: In 1980, after his original house burned in the Agoura Fire of 1978, Hollywood legend Tom Hennesy, stuntman to Rock Hudson and John Wayne, designed and built a new house on a beachfront cliff using wood from two early-nineteenth-century Vermont barns. The stained-glass windows he collected on trips to Ireland. Architect Clive Dawson, who helped Hennesy with the drawings, points out that the framing timber is conventional structural-grade lumber. "I think you'd have a major problem building something like that nowadays," adds Dawson, "because of the code requirements and everything else." OPPOSITE PAGE: Like aspects of the Hennesy House, the handmade aesthetic of Ziza Brown's

three-bedroom, rural Malibu home is decorative. In 2005, Brown, an architectural-salvage expert, antiques collector, and interior designer, acquired an existing fixer-upper and, with only six weeks to complete the work, transformed it inside and out with her "barn loft" concept. Much of the existing woodwork was faux distressed but she also covered entire walls with planks of real barn wood and used barn timbers for focal-point areas like the fireplace. Other prominent surfaces were covered with gray cement ("which I always glaze a bit with very dark brown wax"). Brown says that she had many options for sourcing the barn timber: "I even bought a 30-foot-high two-story barn on eBay for $900. I was quoted $30,000 to take the barn apart and move it from Pennsylvania to Southern California. If you need a large quantity and want to save money, this can be the least expensive way to go. Just be careful it isn't rotten or termite infested. Also, you need to have a contractor or carpenter who's not afraid of it." The lighting and the exposed hardware are also integral

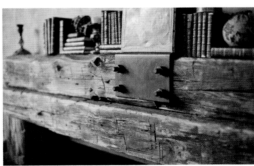

to the look. In the living room, antique
submarine lights hang from copper plumbing
pipe. The electrical wiring is concealed in
more plumbing parts, with each piece objecti-
fied in the overall treatment. The stair was
trimmed with oxidized steel. "I've always
preferred antique hardware but like the
counterpoint of old hardware on very sleek
doors and very contemporary hardware on old
doors," Brown says. "It's always easier to
work with something brand-new but often far
less creative and far more expensive."

British Columbia

In 1963, architect Henry Yorke Mann, an early practitioner of the handmade approach, began a four-year collaboration with Joe and Beth Jankola to expand their existing residence in Burnaby. With several of the city's older houses then being demolished to make way for high-rise apartment buildings, Jankola, also the project's carpenter-builder, had his timber source. As Jankola salvaged more and more wood, Mann revised the drawings. ABOVE, CENTER: For the children's wing, the architect made sure there were child-height windows.

OPPOSITE, BOTTOM: A window wall in the hall-way of the children's wing. OPPOSITE, CENTER RIGHT: The Jankola House entrance had stained glass in the gable ends. OPPOSITE, TOP AND CENTER LEFT: In 1992, Mann began building a house for himself in the Okanagan Valley, with help from mason Gary Klein. Mann's "lawn seat," his meditation place, rests next to the lodgepole pine and concrete-block main house. ABOVE, LEFT: Canada ranks as the world's biggest exporter of forest products, with British Columbia providing half of that output. In the late 1960s, while the wood-butcher movement was beginning to flower on Hornby Island, the island's beaches were at times blanketed with driftwood. When timber was needed, back-to-the-land builders didn't have to go to a commercial lumberyard. Instead, they waited for high tide and went to the beach with a truck and a few friends. ABOVE, RIGHT: Architect and pot-ter Zoltan Kiss started bringing his family to Hornby Island in 1958, well before "the hippie invasion." In the 1970s, he built a beach cottage for himself on Whaling Station Bay, giving the entrance a wall sculpture that pays homage to the island's woodbutcher traditions.

By the time of the Human Be-In celebration
at Vancouver's Stanley Park, on March 26,
1967, finding inroads to the agrarian
ways of old wasn't just a counterculture
preoccupation. In mainstream architecture
circles, even among Modern loyalists, the
old-barn vernacular was becoming a persuasive
image that was too evocative of the prevailing back-to-the-land ideal to ignore. In
1970, on Salt Spring Island, University
of British Columbia Fine Arts Department
director Ian McNairn and a friend, master-
carpenter Aage Villadsen, found a number
of classic old pole barns that were barely
hanging on to life and convinced the owners
to sell the timber. It was the site-honoring
resource that the professor had been seeking for the construction of his own planned
island retreat. Designed by Barry Downs
and Beans Justice of Downs/Archambault &

Partners, a top Vancouver-based Modernist
firm, and built entirely with hand tools by
Villadsen and his son Kent, the 1971 McNairn
House exemplified the new architect-designed
handmade house—a meeting of high art and
folk architectures, with each being better
off for it. In 2003, Bob Dent and Carole
Lycett-Dent became the owners and have since
re-teamed Downs and Kent Villadsen (along
with Villadsen's son John) for a sensitive
restoration and renovation of the original
800-square-foot cottage. OPPOSITE, TOP LEFT:
The McNairn House under construction in 1970.
OPPOSITE, TOP RIGHT: The front elevation
of the original, barn-board-clad McNairn
cottage. OPPOSITE, BOTTOM: A late-nineteenth-
century Salt Spring Island barn. TOP: The
new living room of the McNairn/Dent House.
RIGHT: The original living room with its
sunken seating area.

Midwest, United States

Between the 1920s and '60s, on the Lake
Michigan shores of Charlevoix, Michigan,
builder/developer/realtor and self-taught
architect Earl Young created Boulder Park,
a community characterized by architectural
quirkiness. Although some of Young's designs
echo or exaggerate defining elements of
America's Craftsman style or the cottage-like
vernacular of England's Cotswolds, overall his
houses possess enough daring individuality
to be regarded as part of the handmade house
tradition. Locally sourced Onaway stone was a
favorite, but he also repurposed used conventional materials. Like other designer-builders
in this book, Young approached a house's
design from the roof down. ABOVE: Young's
Half House, built in 1947. RIGHT: A typically
flamboyant Young fireplace in his Weathervane
Terrace Inn and Suites (1965) in Charlevoix.

Vermont

The fantastic Gesundheit Institute for Dr. Patch Adams, the Pitcher Inn, Bridge House—each of these Dave Sellers projects germinated from Tack House, the first building completed for Prickly Mountain. The original four-level split pyramid, a collaboration of architects Sellers, William Reineke, and John Lucas and sculptor Edwin Owre, all friends, was started and finished in 1965, the year Bob Dylan went electric. The budget was tiny but there wasn't a building code. The architects and artists designed it on-site while they were building it. As if this group's open-ended, hands-on process wasn't enough of a challenge to convention, the Yale graduates made the structure using salvage, showcasing parts like rusted, old farm-equipment castings as if they were art objects. It quickly became a curiosity, and in '66, *House Beautiful*, the *New York Times*, and *Progressive Architecture* all published it with marveling enthusiasm. But no one really knew how to categorize Tack House. In fact, it was a classic handmade house—built about five years before that term came into popular use. TOP LEFT: In a stairway inside Tack House, the woodbutcher-style aesthetic is unmistakable. The painting is by Candy Barr. TOP CENTER: Tack House patina. BOTTOM LEFT: The greatly expanded Tack House in 2010, a monument to the design-build movement. ABOVE, RIGHT: The pyramidal volume at left is the original building.

Wales, United Kingdom

In 1972, professor and architect Christopher Day, author of *Places of the Soul: Architecture and Environmental Design as a Healing Art* and a leader of the consensus design movement, restored and renovated a circa 1750 Wesleyan chapel. This was to be his family home. When Day first intervened, he was dealing with a structure that had been overtaken by nature, closed since 1916. Besides the fact that the roof had been removed and used in another building, the chapel's stone walls seemed to be receding into the earth—partly buried, partly concealed under a heavy blanket of ivy and bramble. Over a period of three and a half years, while living in a 9' x 5' chicken coop next door and in between architecture

school teaching stints in London, Day peeled back the layers, resuscitating the ruin like an archaeological dig. Using what stone was already on the property, he reconstructed the walls. He added new "gentle" windows, making them himself. Inside, he incorporated existing boulders into the floor plan, warming it all with new timber framing and other wood features. Save for the fireplace and the stove, he made everything by hand, learning as he went along and without the help of electricity. "I drew very detailed drawings," Day says, "but never looked at them afterward. It evolved as we built it." One of Day's students had introduced him to the turf roofs of his native Norway. The strategy, the professor resolved, made poetic sense in the Welsh landscape and so he followed suit. One day he came home to find a herd of escaped goats grazing atop the house. At that point, he knew he'd gotten the entire project right.

 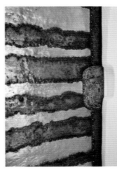 

France

Throughout France there are significant, beautifully sited handmade houses, both historic and contemporary. But on Cavallo, a 100-acre granite outcropping stranded within turquoise and shrouded in mystery between the islands of Corsica and Sardinia, the setting demands the truly exceptional. The cultural tone was set in 1959, when Paris nightclub impresario Jean Castel acquired the island, making it the chosen setting of high-society summer decadence. Still very private today, the "island of billionaires" is said to have 1,000 residents in summer and 10 in winter. Automobiles are forbidden. Thus, instead of the air being filled with fumes, it is perfumed—a mix of black fig, mulberry trees, and the sea. Sardinia resident and artist-architect Savin Couëlle began frequenting the island in the late 1960s, when his "hunter" tendencies led to his being known among the scene's many aristocrats, business titans, artists, and supermodels as "Lupo Bianco," or the "White Wolf." As he recalls of the

period, "The journalists and paparazzi were barred from accessing the island. They were simply thrown back into the sea! It was a fantastic time—nothing to do with the actual concept of life. There was the opportunity of realizing a spontaneous architecture. The madness was sublimated!" Because the best of Couëlle's handmade houses have the presence of a Picasso, his villas were regarded as a status symbol. It was a time of blank checks, boundless creativity, and chilled Negronis sipped lagoonside. TOP: The front elevation of a late-1970s Couëlle villa. ABOVE, RIGHT: The living room of another (earlier) Couëlle villa, this one commissioned by Vittorio Emanuele di Savoia, Prince of Naples, for himself. ABOVE, LEFT: A window of glass block and cullet in the prince's hallway. ABOVE, MIDDLE: A door in the prince's villa. "The houses are made of thousands of details," says Couelle, "like the details in the body of a woman, made of thousands of fascinating surprises."

Italy

TOP LEFT: On the beach in the Costa Smeralda, Sardinia, the iconic Hotel Cala di Volpe, designed in the early 1960s by father and son architects Jacques Couëlle and Savin Couëlle and built by Grassetto of Rome in collaboration with dozens of local craftspeople. Many of the characteristic details seen in the later works of both Couëlles were first formulated for this project. TOP RIGHT: In the early 1960s, during the Aga Khan's initial development of the Costa Smeralda, a model poses next to a handcrafted door of a newly constructed villa. BOTTOM RIGHT: Craftsmen at work during the making of the Costa Smeralda. In the local peasant architecture of old, the twisted, perfumed juniper trunks were temporarily installed to brace a plaster ceiling's construction. In the houses of Savin Couëlle, the juniper is left standing and exposed in the finished building. OPPOSITE, TOP LEFT: Jacques Couëlle in 1966 with a maquette of Monte Mano, the Sardinian residence he designed for himself and wife Veronique. OPPOSITE, CENTER LEFT AND BOTTOM LEFT: In the Hotel Cala di Volpe, a colored glass-block window wall and typical Sardinian ceiling detailing. In the latter, the whitewashed wood of the gable wall is dovetailed and has various Sardinian folk-art etchings. OPPOSITE, TOP RIGHT, BOTTOM RIGHT, AND BOTTOM CENTER: A wall mural at the Albissola Marina house-atelier of the late Danish painter, sculptor, ceramics artist, and CoBrA group founder Asger Jorn. In 1954, after having worked with painter Fernand Léger and architect Le Corbusier, Jorn settled in Albissola Marina, one of Italy's ceramics capitals, to recover from tuberculosis while pursuing his art career. In '57, he and local builder Umberto Gambetta began renovating a decrepit villa that Jorn had acquired with the goal of turning it into the shared home of their two families; eventually nearly every surface of the building and its grounds were accented with paintings and ceramic artworks. While employed at ceramics artist Tullio Mazzotti's studio and local ceramics factories, Jorn salvaged his materials—broken pieces from the floors. Jorn (right) and Gambetta working on a new mural at the villa.

Spain

With much of the handmade house's image
dependent on a revival of peasant or "pioneer" architectures and building arts and
the reuse of materials, the Canary Islands
house of César Manrique fits naturally in
the book. In the 1950s, Manrique was known
throughout Europe as a painter and sculptor,
but in Spain, he was famous. In '68, after
four years of living and making art in New
York City, where he showed at the Catherine
Viviano Gallery and was part of Andy Warhol's
milieu, Manrique returned to his then-
decaying native Lanzarote, the easternmost
island of the Canary chain, and dove into
environmental causes and the preservation of
the local vernacular architecture. Lanzarote,
a stunning geological spectacle of golden
sand dunes and black lava streams, was being
overrun by tourists and overtaken by consum-
erism. "The hour has inevitably come," the
artist said, "to launch a fierce attack on
the devastation of the natural environment
that we are seeing in the Canary Islands, a
destruction which is yet another example of
the atrocities committed against the intel-
ligence of Mother Nature all over the world."
That same year, Manrique began designing and
constructing a house and studio for himself,
a dwelling that quickly became a shining
emblem of his new agendas. The self-trained
architectural designer chose to build atop an
eighteenth-century volcanic eruption, a lava
flow distinguished by deep craters and, most
uniquely and fortuitously, five distinct sub-
terranean bubbles, each large enough to serve
as habitable spaces. Above grade, using only
local materials, he built a series of interconnected structures that echo the island's
peasant tradition, but with modern windows and
reclaimed telephone poles as his timber (the
island has telephone lines but few trees).
From these rooms, stairs spiral down into the
lava bubbles, where he created lounge areas
with built-in furniture. The house's lighting,
another instance of recycling, utilized old
wine jugs and bottles. The carefully preserved
house is now the headquarters of the César
Manrique Foundation.

Australia

Especially in the New South Wales towns of Nimbin and Byron Bay, you can see the back-to-the-land architecture's evolution. There, in the 42 years since the movement made its not-so-subtle arrival and quickly sank its stakes into the earth, a lifestyle that was originally "counterculture" has become decidedly popular. The piecemeal architecture of 1970 and its kindred principles of living off the land were never really ushered away, as they were in parts of the United States. Farther down the coast, in Angourie, it's a similar situation: the handmade house that architecture student John Witzig built for himself around 1972 using junkyard finds is not only still standing and in mostly original condition, but it's up for rent and being marketed in the newspaper as a "historic beach shack." The asking price makes its builder laugh. Witzig, a lauded surfing photographer and journalist, recalls that the movement's earliest enthusiasts were mostly guys like him, local surfers with a global perspective. If Witzig or Garth Murphy or any one of their group ended up surfing in Hawaii or California, for example, typically he'd return home with fuel for the collective fire: a copy of the *Whole Earth Catalog* or *Handmade Houses* or *Shelter*. TOP RIGHT: In 1973, on Cactus Beach near Penong in South Australia, and using whatever materials he could find, architect and former surfing filmmaker Paul Witzig, John's brother, made a place for himself and wife Marianne. LEFT AND BOTTOM: Before and after at John Witzig's handmade house in Angourie.

ORIGINS

"Let me recite what history teaches. History Teaches."

—GERTRUDE STEIN

The antecedents cited by these designers and builders, whether the professionals or the untrained do-it-yourselfers, are wide reaching and add a compelling, unexpected dimension to the story of the handmade house. Some of these individuals talk about the sublime Buddhist architecture of Japan, China, and Tibet. For others, Norway was an irresistible source, particularly architect Knut Knutsen's 1946 handmade cabin on the coast in Portør, a house conceived around salvage and built, as Knutsen put it, in urgent avoidance of "sterile, mechanical repetitions." Some were aware of Henry C. Mercer's Fonthill Castle (1908–12) in Doylestown, Pennsylvania, an early American example of architectural eclecticism and free-hand repurposing, however elaborate. During the Vietnam War draft years, on the West Coast of the United States, many conscientious-objector designers and builders were entirely taken by the modest yet harmonious pioneer and pioneer-style architecture they encountered on their way up through those still-rural regions and into their newly adopted homeland of Canada. Starting in the early 1970s, some found inspiration in the outsider structures created for Dale Chihuly's Pilchuck Glass School in Stanwood, Washington. In these designers' and builders' wholehearted embrace of handcraft as a buffer against the prevailing cultural obsession with all things technologically new, in their mandate to intercept building materials bound for landfills (and spend as little as possible getting them), in their quest for a nurturing, individualistic kind of home amid a world of ever-increasing uniformity, they looked to such houses and other buildings for practical approaches and philosophical guidance. Gathered here are some of those iconic subjects, along with certain well-kept secrets that had escaped discovery, but which now must be acknowledged as essential parts of the handmade house's evolutionary thread.

Charles Lummis

In 1884, the 25-year-old Harvard alum and newspaper editor departed Cincinnati, Ohio, for Los Angeles. He was on foot. Five months and 3,507 miles later, Lummis walked into L.A., where he quickly proceeded to make lasting contributions to California's literary, artistic, and built cultures. In 1896, Lummis started on El Alisal, the house built of river stone that he crafted for himself on the banks of the Arroyo Seco. "The woodwork is massive and all by hand—no mill work," Lummis wrote. "The ceiling beams are 10 x 12" and 8 x 10", all hewn by me with the broad-ax; except two rooms where there are 12-inch cedar logs burned and rubbed. The ceilings are 5-inch redwood, hewn by me with the adze. The casings are massive, no two doors or windows alike; all hewn. Thinnest door three inches thick. Mostly dovetailed. Choice woods. Many historic timbers and other articles built in."

Antoni Gaudí
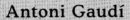

For aspiring architects, Gaudí's Barcelona
is one of the principal stops on "the grand
tour," and even among the general public his
buildings rank among the world's more popular
tourist destinations. It's almost trite to
claim him as an influence; Gaudí belongs to
everyone now. But in the case of the modest
handmade house, Gaudí not only looms, he also
frequently turns up in the DNA test. Consider
the primitivism that he established through
his collagelike application of reclaimed and

found (natural) materials and the buildings'
resulting textures and patinas; or his
unbridled appropriation of ornament (ceramic,
glass, iron, and innumerable exotics), often
purely for sensual effect; or his celebration
of the natural imperfections of the human
touch. "Originality," said Gaudí, "means
going back to our origins." PREVIOUS SPREAD:
In the Colonia Guell Crypt (1898—1915),
a masterpiece made almost entirely from
salvage, Gaudí dressed his mathematically
perplexing structural concept—hyperbolic
paraboloids collide with hyperboloids and
helicoids—in basalt rubble and clinker
brick. To make the grilles for the stained-
and-painted-glass windows, old knitting
needles from Eusebi Guell's textile factory
were collected and sewn together. LEFT:
Casa Batlló (1904—06), Gaudí's great
creative leap. RIGHT: The bench at Park
Guell (1900—1914).

Bernard Maybeck

Bay Area handmade house builders' viewpoint that the process of constructing should essentially be a craft process—the domain of the individual—stems from legendary architect Bernard Maybeck. "With four sticks of wood," Maybeck once remarked, "you can express any emotion." In his many picturesque wood cottages built in and around Berkeley, beginning with his own residence (1892—1902) and carrying on till his final house in 1940, Maybeck emphasized the individual components of the architecture, leaving bare their inherent aesthetic qualities and methods of assemblage. No matter the style employed, the designs tended to leave the structure exposed. In the 1960s, the region's woodbutchers sparked a rediscovery of Maybeck's work and, in their own houses, picked up where he'd left off. LEFT: A later design, the 1933 Wallen Maybeck House, built in Berkeley for the architect's son and his wife. The dining area shows the exposed structure typical of his houses. The sand-blasted truss timbers are joined with decorative steel plates. TOP: The Grove Clubhouse, 1903, the Russian River cabin designed for San Francisco's Bohemian Club. BOTTOM: Maybeck's first house, the building described in Charles Keeler's 1904 book *The Simple Home* as "distinctly hand-made."

Charles Greene

At first the highly refined houses of Arts and Crafts architects Greene & Greene seem to be at odds with the defining criteria of the handmade house, especially that movement's improvisational style and rough-hewn texture expressed in found materials. But handmade-house builders' frequent citing of Greene & Greene as inspiration points to the philosophical link between these two movements—one from the nineteenth century and the other from the 1960s, and both sharing in a rejection of the machine-made. In Charles Greene's later solo work, there's a literal connection. His 1923 house/studio in Carmel was crafted with scrap lumber and brick from a demolished hotel, and he salvaged marble left over from the 1922 James House (TOP). RIGHT: A plaster wall in the house/studio has stencil work by Charles Greene, all done in avoidance of uniformity. LEFT: The front door of the famous Gamble House (1908), by Greene & Greene.

Robinson Jeffers

In his verse, Jeffers repeatedly visited his archetypal handmade house, so much so that to his readers it may seem possible to see the home's artifact-embedded walls through the poet's eyes. Jeffers was 32 when in May of 1919 he accepted M. J. Murphy's $2,230 bid to build a small stone residence for the family's new barren acreage at Carmel Point. An unrelenting environmentalist, Jeffers wasn't a builder, at least not then. But throughout the three months spent completing the redwood-and-sea-stone Tor House, the poet was on the job—setting and sculpting as an apprentice to mason Robert Pearson. In 1920, on his own, he fearlessly embarked on building the 40-foot-tall Hawk Tower. In El Alisal, the home of his early publisher, Charles Lummis, you find the root of Jeffers's narrative. BOTTOM LEFT: Pre-Columbian terra-cotta heads are among the hundreds of details with which Jeffers personalized the construction.

Carl Jung

During the late 1960s and early '70s, the period of the handmade house's codification—what was for many of its designers and builders a time of introspective reevaluation and outward defiance of broken social and political codes—the work of Carl Gustav Jung became a guiding force. (Jung's concept of individuation in effect summarizes the very stimulus that resulted in the handmade house phenomenon.) The semiautobiography of the Swiss psychiatrist and founder of analytical psychology, *Memories, Dreams, Reflections*, was first published in 1962 and was revised in '73, but by the time of its original publication, Jung had already built his handmade house on Lake Zurich, the complex of structures known as Bollingen Tower. Jung's tower evolved piecemeal, like so many other handmade houses, starting in 1923 and extending into the 1950s. And like other designer-builders, in the many details of his design and construction work he could see his own idiosyncrasies.

Edgar Miller

In 1928, a year ahead of the Great Depression, on Chicago's North Shore, two former Art Institute classmates were scouring demolition sites and bribing junk dealers in search of building materials for their new real estate venture. Sol Kogen, recently departed from his family's silk business, and Edgar Miller, a prodigious stained-glass artist, had partnered in the renovation of a run-down three-story Victorian apartment building on what's now Burton Place. Kogen's idea was to transform it into the eclectic kind of studios that he'd seen in Paris's Montmartre. Miller, who already had hands-on remodeling experience and could work in practically any medium, was to provide the creative. As they accumulated Victorian brick, tile, wrought iron, oak doors and ceiling beams, marble, and copper kitchen and bath components, Kogen and Miller improvised the building's 17 units. While Miller was busy with his carvings, stained glass, ceramics, and frescoes for each handmade apartment, Kogen addressed the probing of building inspectors—offers of drawn portraits usually were enough to get them to overlook any violations. But before the pair had even completed that work, Kogen had wheeled and dealed them into a second building, on Wells Street. Miller somehow kept up, and his achievements in the nine-unit Wells building, completed circa 1932, show a genius that is only now being rediscovered and appreciated. LEFT: The living room at the Wells Street Glasner Studio. RIGHT: A Wells Street façade.

Douglas Ellington

To build his Asheville, North Carolina, residence, École des Beaux Arts—trained architect Douglas Ellington excused himself from the fashionable intellectual pursuits of his profession and created purely from the heart. Ellington House (1926—31) ended up an improvised quilt of architect's samples, countryside salvage scores, and landfill-destined odds and ends rescued by Ellington from his simultaneous Asheville projects, the Art Deco—style City Building and Asheville High

School. Ellington, his draftsmen, and a group of mountain men did the labor, all without electricity. "Douglas was an urgent recycler, a natural-born recycler," said Ellington's niece, wildlife artist Sallie Ellington Middleton. "He couldn't stand waste of any kind." ABOVE RIGHT: The living room's axe-hewn beams came out of an abandoned Weaverville schoolhouse. The ceiling's boards had been concrete formwork elsewhere. The window grille was a high school building leftover.

Scott & Helen Nearing

The onetime economist and his musician wife's subsistence-living experiment in Vermont, all of it chronicled in *Living the Good Life* (1954), turned out to be brilliantly fore-telling. When Scott and Helen left New York City in 1932, she was 28 but he was 50. In the country, as they had been in the city, they proved to be rigidly self-disciplined, hyperefficient, and frequently ahead of the cultural curve. By the arrival of the back-to-the-land movement and its adoption of them as figureheads, the couple was 15 years strong into their second homesteading adventure, on the Maine coast. In 1970, *Living the Good Life* was rushed back into print. TOP LEFT: The Nearings' Vermont houses are there today, each privately owned. When you walk into Forest Farm, you can't help but flash back to their description of it from '54: "One entered directly into a roomy kitchen, low of ceiling, with exposed hand-hewn raf-ters, brown-stained paneling, wood stove and a pine plank table under broad windows facing the mountain. In the whole house there was to be no wallpaper, plastering or paint. Furniture of the simplest was to be home-made and built in wherever possible." The building is a handmade house template. BOTTOM LEFT: Their first Vermont cabin, an opportunity to learn architect Ernest Flagg's "mosaic rubble" technique. ABOVE, RIGHT: 1938-1943, Nearing designed and built Forest Farm, the outcome of Helen's "childish" rendering of a Swiss chalet-style farmhouse.

Sam Trotter

A Sam Trotter post-and-beam house made of hand-split redwood is an image that every good Big Sur carpenter knows. Active in the 1920s and '30s (when the area saw many new houses added to its assortment of homesteads), Trotter was Big Sur's premier early designer-builder. His big break was the 1925 redwood-log lodge for the Santa Lucia Trails Club, what's now a private part of the Nepenthe restaurant complex. In 1944, actor-director Orson Welles had acquired the Trails Club log house as a gift for his new wife, actress Rita Hayworth. Little known outside the community, he didn't so much blaze new trails as carry forward the tried and true, reaffirming its importance to the sense of place. At a time when Modernism's factory-made metallic luster was breaking out in cities all around him, Trotter was in the Santa Lucia mountains felling and splitting redwood for houses that would be made entirely by hand. In his iconic cabins around Big Sur, including his collaborations with Bay Area architect William Wurster, you see the hand-hewn source material for much of what became the West Coast's woodbutcher style. TOP LEFT: Hangover Hut, 1928. TOP RIGHT: Mucha Vista, 1937. ABOVE: R.J. Davis House, 1934.

Helmuth Deetjen

In 1936, Helmuth Deetjen and his future wife, Helen Haight, traded a house in Carmel for a tent on 3.95 acres in Big Sur, intending on building a new home. By '41, with help from investor Barbara Blake, they'd completed five structures and turned the property into the Big Sur Inn. In the making of these early buildings, the self-taught carpenter developed the charm-loaded look—more nineteenth-century California ranch than the painted-clapboard vernacular of his native Bergen, Norway—that would not only inform what the inn has become today but also inspire countless builders of handmade houses who happened to stop by. Exposed redwood post-and-beam framing, single-wall redwood board-and-bat sheathing, low ceilings and concrete floors, reclaimed small-paned windows, hand-carved porch balusters, and homemade wrought-iron hardware are the staple ingredients. Some of the redwood lumber that Deetjen used he salvaged from Monterey canneries.

Bruce Goff

Information on Bruce Goff and his 147-odd buildings is not hard to come by, especially his most famous work, Bavinger House (1950), but this doesn't stop his work from being misunderstood—presented as mid-century Modern or other oddly formal classification. In fact, when Goff, a self-taught architect, taught architecture at the University of Oklahoma in the 1940s and '50s, he forbid his students from using *any* existing architectural style. It had to be born from the situation at hand.

Once, when a student wanted to design a Gothic cathedral, Goff reprimanded: "You don't have a Gothic mind!" Many designers and builders of handmade houses found freedom in Goff's plant- and animal-like forms, his circular and suspended plans, his view that ornament should be used uninhibitedly as a personalizing device, and his total endorsement of found materials. ABOVE: Goff's Cole House (1939) in Park Ridge, Illinois. The front door had windows made from ashtrays.

Alexander Weygers

The sculptor, blacksmith, carpenter, engineer, printer, engraver, photographer, inventor, teacher, and author had to have been the envy of every artist who crossed his path. Weygers seemingly could do it all, and while doing it he spent much time living off the land. In 1943 he and his wife, Marian, also an artist, moved to Carmel Valley and began building the home studio (ABOVE) that they would occupy for the next five decades and routinely share with visitors. Nearly every object in the house Weygers made himself. Besides its curvaceous form, the structure was exceptional for its materials: reclaimed Monterey pine-slab cladding, a mushroom-like adobe roof, salvaged windows and doors, and beautiful hardware that he forged from auto-junkyard finds. "There's a fine line between what we want and what we need," Weygers said. "If you make what you need, you may find that it's also what you want."

OPEN-AIR RESTAURANT
exploits the beauty of a hilltop site overlooking the Pacific

Rowan Maiden & the Trotter Bros.

Several of Big Sur's most soulful older heavy-timber houses are the work of Walter Trotter and Frank Trotter, sons and apprentices of Sam Trotter. The Trotter brothers were involved in the making of Wild Bird (1955–58), the widely published Big Sur home of Nathaniel and Margaret Owings. But among builders of handmade houses, their most influential work is the landmark restaurant Nepenthe, a substantial addition to a 1925 log cabin (built by their father) that they started on in '48 with architect Rowan Maiden and new owners Bill and Lolly Fassett. Maiden, a former Frank Lloyd Wright apprentice, had sold the Fassetts on an open-plan design that depended on the kind of exposed trusswork that Wright had employed at Taliesin West. Using locally milled rough-sawn Big Sur redwood, the Trotters met the challenge of Maiden's drawings. LEFT, TOP AND BOTTOM: In 1960, *Architectural Digest* applauded Nepenthe. ABOVE: Nepenthe in the 1950s.

Sea Ranch

Only a year after *Silent Spring*, the 1962 book that had practically the entire country talking about the environment, and well ahead of the California Coastal Commission's founding, a corporate developer daringly launched a planned community on several thousand environmentally sensitive acres, a former sheep farm, along Northern California's desolate Sonoma coast. Called Sea Ranch, the development's original creative team included landscape architect Lawrence Halprin, the architecture firms of Joseph Esherick & Associates and Moore Lyndon Turnbull Whitaker (MLTW), and builder Matthew Sylvia. Today, nearly 50 years after its ground breaking, Sea Ranch continues to thrive, and while it hasn't been exempt from controversy, it's generally held up as an exemplar of ecologically sensitive place making. MLTWs tone-setting first Sea Ranch building, a 10-unit condominium, took much of its dialect from local barns and from the nearby historic Russian settlement Fort Ross. The condo's timber-frame structures were clad with vertically hung redwood boards and roofed with redwood shingles, all left bare. This wasn't just an exterior treatment used to harmonize the buildings with their rural setting though. Says architect Donlyn Lyndon, "We determined that the structure of the building should be an active element—that it should not be hidden away as little wood studs concealed behind plasterboard." Influencing the decision to leave the wood structure entirely exposed on the interior, he says, were the interiors of the Big Sur Inn. Perfectly evocative of its site, the condo became a sensation. Besides shifting the values systems of design tastemakers and Modern loyalists worldwide, this one building was many an architect's "way in" to woodbutcher-style design and construction, their key to the handmade house. TOP LEFT: MLTW's Condominium One, 1965. TOP RIGHT AND BOTTOM: The Brunsell House, 1987, by architect Obie Bowman. The fireplace was made with salvaged clinker bricks.

Mr. Lloyd House

Before 1968, the year Vancouver designer-builder Lloyd House landed on Hornby Island, the local architecture didn't provide an incentive for visitors to make the extended trek required to access the remote island from the mainland. That changed with the driftwood-and-plaster Ngan Studio (1968), a collaboration between House, potter Wayne Ngan, and Ngan's then-wife, Ann, a weaver and painter. House's second project, a Zen-inspired hut surrounded by drippy coastal woods, was the island's architectural sonic boom, however, the tone setter for the wood-butcher movement that was about to flourish there. Commissioned by a University of British Columbia professor of Buddhist studies, House was given a budget of $2,500. While on the property to determine the cabin's exact site, he had the kind of experience that every builder dreams of: In the still air, a fallen maple leaf came fluttering down to the ground in front of him, landing flat atop a few blades of grass. "The leaf had rested," House says, "and I thought, 'there's the roof.'" For House, the roof is always built first, and it dictates much of the rest. The rest he let happen in keeping with "the spirit and the energy" that had gotten him that far. TOP AND BOTTOM: Leaf House (1969). House dreamed up a lightweight leaflike roof made of three layers of ½-inch laminated cedar and a driftwood-log ridge beam, all ingeniously dependent on a single driftwood post. The built-ins are also driftwood.

ARCHITECTURE *without* ARCHITECTS

Emile Norman & Brooks Clement

c. 1950-80

EMILE NORMAN, the California artist whose organic-themed works in sculpture and the decorative arts were nothing if not meticulously designed, used to say that the greatest designer of all was Baroque composer Johann Sebastian Bach. "Bach could take me way out into outer space. But he always had a resolution. He always brought me back down," the artist remarked in his home studio, where he had achieved the very same feat. In the 59

ABOVE: Brooks Clement (left) and Emile Norman
in the original living room in the 1950s.
The low wall bears a Norman mosaic sculpture
of a dry-riverbed scene, a meaningful image
from the artist's childhood. Displayed behind
his chair is one of the artist's classic
multipaneled foliage screens—work for which
he received an important commission from *House
Beautiful* editor Elizabeth Gordon in the '60s.

Emile Norman's once-simple
redwood box on Big Sur's
Pfeiffer Ridge, originally
built in 1950 by Walter
Trotter, morphed repeatedly
in Norman's time there.
Personalized down to the
last beautifully articulated
detail, Norman's home became
the embodiment of his evolution as an artist—a virtual
self-portrait. THIS PAGE:
The solarium elevation. The
flagpole stems from the
lookout tower—a balcony seat
for whale watching, sunset
viewing, and star sighting.

years that Norman resided in the house that he and his life partner and business manager, Brooks Clement, had built on Big Sur's Pfeiffer Ridge, the house had been repeatedly transformed. Most of that work they had done themselves. As his art gained in value, the house grew both in size and embellishment. It's got "outer-space" gestures that speak of the artist's fun-loving flamboyancy. It's got calming understatement, another of his personality traits. As a whole, it's his richest, most complex work. When Norman died in September 2009 at 91 years old, he left behind a house that's a lot like Bach's famous Goldberg Variations: the more you look for artful detail and richness of expression in it, the more you find.

OUT OF SORTS

Even by 1946 standards, they weren't making good time. By midnight, Emile Norman and Brooks Clement had ridden out several hours of blinding rain and fog in their quest to get up the coast from Los Angeles to their new residence in Big Sur. Finally, Clement took the hard left off the old coastal corridor, US Highway 1, that linked to their property. He didn't get far on the unlit gravel road before he abruptly hit the brakes. In the moonlight he could see a fast-overflowing Big Sur River where there should've been a bridge. If the span was there at all, they couldn't be sure. For now, there would be no getting home, at least not without help.

Weeks earlier, they had met Walter Trotter, a local builder and rancher who was known for his ability to deal with the area's unique challenges. Trotter had told the new locals, both of them then in their late 20s, to call on him if they ever needed a hand. Within an hour they were knocking on the door of Trotter's

house at the Fuller Ranch. "My mom and dad welcomed them right in," says Trotter's son, Michael, "and they all sat around talking and drinking hot chocolate until about six in the morning." By daybreak, Trotter had the young men safely across the bridge—and home.

SETTLING IN

By 1950, Norman and Clement had settled in and were expanding their holdings in the area. They'd acquired a 120-acre tract of Pfeiffer Ridge, a timber claim that had belonged to Walter Trotter's aunt, Florence Pfeiffer, and her late husband, John Pfeiffer. As a site for construction, the ridge was a blank canvas. It also had uninterrupted ocean views. Having outgrown their small riverside cabin in the lowland redwoods, it was decided that they would build a new house on their new land, a place with a proper studio where Emile could work. Once again, Norman and Clement called on Trotter.

The Pfeiffer Ridge land acquisition, a deal made for about $6,000, had the couple financially in a bind. With the help of Trotter's expertise and friendship, however, Norman and Clement would get their house. Trotter, who, with his older brother and frequent building partner, Frank, was just finishing the construction of architect Rowan Maiden's widely

OPPOSITE: In the late 1960s, in order to accommodate their new Johannes Klais pipe organ, the couple expanded the living room—a project done with more Big Sur redwood and credited to Horst Mayer. As a gift to Clement, an exceptional keyboard player, Norman crafted a case for the instrument. Their dinner parties, attended by the likes of Julia Child and Michael Tilson Thomas, were never the same.

published design for Nepenthe restaurant in Big Sur. By comparison, the new project would be a much more modest affair, at least to start.

A ROOF OVERHEAD

The original building was a rudimentary two-story live/work space, a 40' x 60' shell with the potential for modification and enhancement. The floor plan consisted of a studio and a workshop on the lower level and, upstairs, the living space. Norman, Clement, and Trotter installed a kitchen and a bathroom, but

otherwise the living area was left entirely open and loftlike. Local redwood milled at nearby Big Creek, now a nature reserve, made up the framework and the exterior cladding. For the floors, Trotter used 6-inch tongue-and-groove Douglas fir planks; for the ceilings, 1½-inch redwood lath.

It was built in the cheapest way possible and in no more than 60 days. Michael Trotter, who, besides being the son of the builder, has been caretaking the property since 1972, says, "It was done very quickly, with a very simple layout. They rolled the floor joists, they put the flooring down, and they framed the

outside edge of the thing and nailed the siding to it. Then they put a roof on it, put the windows in it, and Brooks and Emile moved in. That was it." Trotter remembers hearing that the construction's informality and expediency was in keeping with the area's permit process: "When Emile went into town to get a permit, they told him, 'Ah, hell, down in Big Sur you don't need a permit to build a house.'"

EXPANSIONS

Once they were moved in, Norman's career quickly took off. In '51, he had a show of animal sculptures and nature-inspired figures at New York's Feingarten Gallery. In '53, he completed a number of his signature nature-themed resin panels for the American President Lines cruise ships. In '55, Norman was awarded a commission to create a four-story window for a Masonic temple in San Francisco. Before it had even been finished, the Masons expanded his contribution to include a similarly large-scale marble sculpture for the building's façade. The Mason project, completed in 1958, made the artist $100,000 richer. As always, he poured much of the income into the house. "He was on such a big success wave through the '50s," says Jeff Mallory, trustee of the Emile Norman Charitable Trust. "There was no limit to ideas for what he wanted to build."

Norman was always experimenting with materials and reimagining their potential uses. His sink-side kitchen cabinet doors are linoleum over redwood, designed to fold accordion-like to maximize his workspace. (Norman loved to cook.) The room's oak floor is ornamented with copper nails—each painstakingly pre-drilled and hammered by property caretaker Michael Trotter. More of Norman's wood-inlay pieces hang by the passage.

To cut costs, the original wing of the house,
containing the dining area, was built like a
loft. Later on, instead of putting up walls,
Norman used cabinets of his design and
construction to partition the spaces. For
greater light penetration and a heightened
sense of expansiveness room to room, he
didn't take the modules to the ceiling.
The table is his, as are the hanging works.

"A lot of the artists would come to Big Sur
because it was known as an artistic headquarters,"
Norman stated in 2005. "Some stayed and some
didn't. I stayed." By that time, the house that he and
Clement had eagerly moved into in 1950 had long
since disappeared—overtaken by expansion in nearly
every direction. Early on, Norman had crafted
dividers to section off the functions—bedroom,

living room, and dining room—but more space was
always needed. The 1950s were a period of various
renovations and expansions. Most of these were
artistic, like the wall near the living room fireplace
that displays a cast-concrete sculpture depicting a
riverbed scene. During this same time, Norman also
began designing and building furniture for the house,
often from leftover or otherwise reclaimed wood.

In 1962, Walter Trotter was again constructing
additions to the home. By this time, most of the
house's decks had been enclosed and made a part of
the interior living space, with the weathered wood

from the exterior left exposed to contribute to the overall patina. In a major kitchen renovation, Norman used materials left over from the Masonic temple project, casting the kitchen countertops in flaming gold leaf for the cooking section, and cooler pastel shades for the sink section—another marriage of art and function. In '67, it was a swimming pool. For that project, Trotter had salvaged a 5,000-gallon redwood water tank and cut it to a depth of 5 feet. Clement couldn't swim.

Further additions included a solarium, a guest bedroom, covered and uncovered decks, access ramps, a lookout tower, a new studio, and, perhaps most significantly, a double-height room for the pipe organ they'd acquired in Zurich, Switzerland. Norman crafted the instrument's singular casework. As the house grew, the building materials usually got richer—most of it rare or exotic woods and other materials leftover from Norman's sculpture work and other art projects. The wood was always minimally finished so its inherent beauty could shine.

TO BE CONTINUED

Even in his late 80s, Norman was working on the house. "Emile's mind was always working," says Michael Trotter. "He always kept a pad and pencil next to him. He'd have a dream in the middle of the night and would wake up and start sketching—his artwork or something he was thinking about doing on the house. He might start it tomorrow or he might start it in six months."

During the making of the 2006 PBS documentary film *Emile Norman: By His Own Design*, Norman, age 91, led the film crew on a tour of his home, explaining to yet another group of admiring guests all the work he and partner Brooks Clement had done to it over

Wood is the dominant material in Norman's vast body of work, and often he sourced exotic species. Never one to waste leftovers (he even stockpiled and reused sawdust), he tended to find use for them in his house. A cabinet in the hall beyond the kitchen has a plant-motif inlay done with several kinds of wood. Typical of the artist, the detail is given inconspicuous placement.

the years. "I think the house reflects love," Norman told them. "It was built by two people that were very compatible. He was a wonderful electrician and plumber. And I did all of the cabinetwork. And it just kept growing. All handmade. And I think it's almost finished now. Not quite, but almost."

EMILE NORMAN HOUSE. Big Sur, California.
Walter Trotter, architectural designer and builder.
Emile Norman, interior and furniture designer.

James & Anne Hubbell

c. 1958-2007

THE "DREAM HOUSE." If you could build yours, what would it look like? In designing it in your mind, could you resist tradition and convention and let your imagination run free? While transferring the idea to paper and getting it built, could you stay true to the purity of your original intent? Would you be so daring as to try? In the summer of 1958, artist James Hubbell and his wife, Anne, a first-grade teacher, parked a borrowed trailer on their 10 acres in the remote mountainous backcountry east of San Diego, rolled up their sleeves, and committed themselves to doing just that.

A month earlier, the newlyweds had been living at home with their parents. In the yard of his mother's Rancho Santa Fe residence, Hubbell had built himself a small studio. But, otherwise, the young sculptor, like his wife, had no residential design and construction experience. They'd gotten together the $3,500 to buy the Wynola land but the surplus ended there. Money was as tight as you'd expect on the incomes of a teacher and a struggling artist. Could the couple, then only in their 20s, have come up with a bolder start to their lives together?

What they lacked in experience and financial resources the Hubbells made up for in determination and, in James's case, extraordinary artistic ability. In '62, although work on

the house was still incomplete, they gave up the trailer and the frequent commutes to and from San Diego and moved in. For the next three decades, while raising four Hubbell boys and devoting part of their week to day jobs (he was making art; she was teaching school), James and Anne continued on the project. He designed everything, and she helped him build it. The scrounging for and reclaiming of materials, the spreading of mortar, the rough

James Hubbell didn't shy away from the freedom afforded him by his site's isolation (elevation 3,500 feet). The structures that make up his environment are as much "works of art" as anything else he's made with his hands—so much so that it's easy to forget he also calls them home. OPPOSITE: A trellis's carved cedar post helps frame a perspective of the pool and the sculpted living/dining/kitchen wing. Note the pool and roof mosaics, the deliberate placement of the large hunk of turquoise cullet, and the forged-iron handrails. ABOVE: James and Anne Hubbell near their courtyard fireplace, 2010.

electrical work—they did it all themselves. To get the necessary engineering for his designs, Hubbell would reach out to friends like architect Kendrick Kellogg, often trading one of his artworks for the services. Occasionally the couple's friends made the long drive out to Wynola for "rock parties" and other work-oriented get-togethers, the extra hands helping them with the heavy lifting. Even the kids in attendance contributed, gathering rocks in their little red wagons and depositing them at the construction site.

By the late 1980s, the Hubbells were finally starting to see their home as being "done." Little by little, and without ever taking out a loan, they'd built their dream house. In fact, by that point they'd built seven of them on the property. When they could afford to build more, they usually did. "If I was low on money," James says, "I could always afford a bag of cement and lay stone."

There was never a master plan for the individual buildings that make up this live/work compound, the heart of a foundation that they call Ilan-Lael, Hebrew for "a tree belonging to God." "From each building," says Hubbell, "I could learn things and then I could play with them and then take it to the next. Each building has kind of a different language that I was interested in at the time. When I work on something, a place has its own identity. It's like a friend." There was a certain process, however. Most of the time, the structures began as clay models and the architectural forms evolved from them. "I do clay models all the time," Hubbell says, "and I find that my hands do things. And then I look at it and I say, 'Well, that looks like what I wanted to do.' "

FOUNDATIONAL JOURNEYS

Although the singularity of his art, architecture, and other designs suggests otherwise, James Hubbell isn't entirely self-taught. In 1951, he attended the Whitney Art School in New Haven, Connecticut. In '54, following two years in the US Army during the Korean War, he enrolled at Cranbrook Academy of Art in Bloomfield Hills, Michigan. There, Hubbell majored in sculpture and minored in painting and metalsmithing. In the 1950s he was also traveling extensively on his own, exploring and making paintings of what he saw. By '57, he had logged nearly four years abroad—England, Spain, Italy, France, Korea, Japan, and parts of Africa included. During this time he spent almost a year in Europe, "wandering," he says from one cathedral to another. Stained glass quickly became one of his obsessions.

While in Spain, Hubbell visited various works by Antoni Gaudí, some of which would have a lasting influence on him. The highlight, he says, was the Catalonian architect's Colonia Güell crypt in Santa Coloma de Cervelló. "I think that when I saw the crypt I realized you could do buildings that were sculptural. Most of his buildings are façades. . . . But with that one, he's really handling the building as if it were sculpture."

In late 1957, after Hubbell had returned from his travels and settled at his mother's house in Rancho Santa Fe, a family friend in nearby Del Mar commissioned him for a stained glass window. That piece

OPPOSITE: The reconstructed living/dining/kitchen wing, built using reclaimed cedar and incorporating the original fireplace, displays multiple examples of Hubbell's lighting designs. The sofa and chair are by Del Cover. The side table is a Michael Creely.

and other works shown at his one-person show that year at the Museum of Contemporary Art San Diego were seen by prominent local architect Sim Bruce Richards. An apprentice to Frank Lloyd Wright in 1934 and '35 and an accomplished furniture designer, weaver, and painter, Richards immediately took to Hubbell's nature-inspired creations. Their meeting led to a friendship, and for the next 20-plus years Richards and Hubbell fed off each other's creativity, appreciation for nature, and love of building. "You know, architects don't hire artists," says Hubbell. "But every house Bruce did, he had me do stuff. It gave me an income. Without Bruce, I wouldn't be doing this work."

IN HIS NATURE

Were you to take a walk through a forest with James Hubbell, you'd begin to acquire a new appreciation for the trees, the plants, the soil, the innumerable species that make up that habitat, and how the sun energizes it all. That's his world. Since childhood, the artist says, nature has been the one place where he's always felt comfortable. Hubbell's single mother raised him, and as they moved frequently, by the time he was 12 he'd been in and out of as many schools. "When I was a kid, I really didn't understand adults very well. But I did understand and feel very at home with nature. When I grew up, I lived quite a bit near

forests, and I think it really helped me because it gave me the sense that there was magic."

As a designer and builder, Hubbell continually finds his way back to that extraordinary feeling—the "magic" that he discovered as a child. His John Muir–like perception, awareness, and appreciation of the natural world radiates from the forms and the material textures in his work. It's present in each of the buildings that make up his house.

"I wish that man could live in homes as marvelous and beautiful as those of the snail," Hubbell told the *Los Angeles Times* in 1968, "and that he could build cities as endlessly rewarding as the forest." In 2011, at 80 and with his work very much ongoing, he still sees it that way.

BIODIVERSITY

One late-spring morning in 2004, James and Anne were having breakfast in the sun at a small table on the east-facing patio outside the Boys' House, the building Hubbell built in 1973 for his sons a short walk from his own bedroom. This is the most sculptural, the most fantastical of all the buildings on the Hubbell property. Hidden beneath the unusual structure's thin layer of texturized cement is a framework of 2-inch pipe covered with rebar and metal lath. To give the structural pipes their curved shapes, Hubbell would heat each one and then place it in the crotch of a tree, bending it with his weight. Portions of the curved walls, inside and out, are filled in with broken pieces of adobe brick, granite picked up from around the site, and glass cullet in a range of colors. Several of the buildings here were made this way. It's the link, Hub-

bell's homage, to Gaudí's Colonia Güell crypt. What separates the Boys' House from those other Hubbell structures, though, is the degree to which he sculpted the interior space. Just as he would have done in the planning stages with a clay model, during the construction the artist carved out each of the rooms. Even the doors are framed without right angles. Every inch of the grottolike interior architecture appears to have been worked by hand with artistic intention.

After the building became liveable, Hubbell took another three years adding layers. To comprehend the amount of detail in just the bathroom could fill several pleasure-filled hours. The room has one of his leaded stained glass skylights and windows and one of his famous doors with intricate carvings and leaded stained glass inlay, all done in a floral motif. This particular one is redwood, like the room's vanity cabinet. On the shower wall, in a range of flora and fauna motifs, he created a symphony of mosaic, granite, cullet, dull-edge shards of panel glass, and abalone shells. Oval pieces of polished cullet cradled in hand-forged metal, again crafted by Hubbell, serve as the faucet and cabinet handles.

But, in 2004, the Boys' House became home to James and Anne. The previous October, while on a flight to San Diego from New York, they looked out the plane window and saw smoke billowing from the vicinity of their property. The Cedar Fire, the largest fire in recorded history in California, was at that very moment closing in on their home. For the next day and a half, the Hubbell family raced to remove what they could from the buildings. But then the fire took control. When it was over, four of the eight buildings of their compound, including their living/dining/kitchen and master-bedroom buildings, had been gutted. Only the buildings' walls, chimneys, and other stonework

The incomparable Boys' House, built in 1973 for Hubbell's sons.
"At about 14," says Hubbell, laughing, "our son Drew moved
here, before the doors and windows were even on. He just took
his suitcase and his records and left home." Steps extend the
recreation area to the rooftop.

portions were left standing amid the piles of ash. "I'm determined not to let it ruin the rest of my life," Hubbell told a *Los Angeles Times* reporter in the immediate aftermath. "I'm not going to give it my misery. We have a lot of friends, which is sometimes more important than money. Most times." Considering that Hubbell had stored all his art and materials in a few of those burned buildings, the losses were almost incalculable. By chance, the Boys' House had survived mostly intact.

Right away, the Hubbell family and their many friends pushed to resurrect the fire-damaged structures. For the rebuild, partially burned cedar trees from the area were milled into useable lumber. Bits and pieces of heirlooms and other objects that had not been entirely damaged in the fire, such as the plates that Ann had inherited from her parents and various kinds of Hubbell-made wrought-iron hardware, were recycled into the new construction. Drew

Hubbell, the couple's eldest son and the architect in Hubbell & Hubbell Architects, contributed to the renovation and restoration and helped to greatly improve the original buildings' energy efficiency and fire resistance. Builder and reclaimed-materials expert Mark Tighe tirelessly brought his expertise. By Christmas 2006, the Herculean reconstruction effort was far enough along for James and Anne to return to their bedroom and their living/dining/kitchen buildings.

OPEN HEART, OPEN DOORS

Every year, the Hubbells share Ilan-Lael with the public for a day. The property operates as a foundation, providing "a quiet place for public reflection of how art, nature and beauty connect to our lives and our actions in the wider world." This year, demand for tickets is higher than ever, and so they've increased the number of tours. In keeping with the way the house was built, the event is designed to be a family affair. Anne Hubbell, the former first-grade teacher, is always especially eager to welcome kids to their home. "We like children to see our handmade house," she says, "so that they know that there are other possibilities than living in just the boxes that we're given by commercial enterprises." One such visitor, a little boy, managed to summarize perfectly the beauty of this house in a thank-you note he later sent to the Hubbells: "Mr. Hubbell makes houses that trees aren't embarrassed to stand next to."

ILAN-LAEL. Wynola, California. James Hubbell, architectural designer, builder, and principal artist and craftsperson.

OPPOSITE: The Boys' House interior with its lower-level and loft sleeping areas and kitchenette/living area. The chandelier of forged iron and glass is also by Hubbell.
ABOVE: The sky-lit Boys' House bathroom, where taking a bath during a full moon is nothing less than a joyful transformative experience.

The beautiful rawness of what J.B. Blunk built is the same *shibui* aesthetic that
he discovered in the 1950s upon moving in with Isamu Noguchi when the famous
sculptor was residing at Rosanjin Kitaōji's 200-year-old farmhouse in Kamakura,
Japan. Partially devoted to exhibiting the artist's furniture, paintings,
and sculpture, this space was originally the Blunk family's open living area/
master bedroom, with only a sofa and a beaded curtain lending the adults privacy.
The ladder goes to the children's sleeping loft, where the beds were hand-cut
slabs of industrial foam, never actual mattresses. OPPOSITE: The Blunk family at
home in the early 1960s: Rufus, Bruno, Nancy, and J.B.

J.B. Blunk &
Nancy Waite

c. 1960

SCULPTORS ISAMU NOGUCHI and J.B. Blunk and Surrealist painter Gordon Onslow Ford were standing together in the shadows of a thousand Bishop pines, taking in the crisp air and the cloud breaks and admiring the undisturbed beauty of the rolling landscape—land that Onslow Ford was preparing to acquire. On those 250 acres in Inverness, California, the painter intended to start an artist's colony. It was late 1956. The news of Onslow Ford's intentions came at a turning point for the 29-year-old Blunk. Newly married to artist Nancy Waite, he was about to start a family, and he had recently relocated from Los Angeles to the Bay Area and was trying to find his groove. He was making pottery and jewelry but, more than anything else, he was struggling financially. Work as a camp counselor and as a hand on a sheep ranch

in Mendocino County, near Fort Ross, gave some much-needed cash. What he really needed, though, was a break with his art. Noguchi was aware of his friend's predicament. They'd been close since their meeting in Japan in '52, where Blunk had even lived with him for a period. Noguchi's way of helping Blunk now was connecting him with Onslow Ford. It was a move that would forever alter the young artist's life.

SOUTHERLY EXPOSED

Before he'd even built for himself on the Inverness property, Onslow Ford gave Blunk his pick of land—an acre on which to create a live/work environment. "Gordon really took to J.B.," says Waite. "He sort of had a place in mind for us but it was a little bit not what we were hoping for. So he said, 'Go find your own.' We walked the property and found a place, and we decided that it was *the* place. It had a southern exposure and gorgeous views." The couple got started. At Waite's suggestion, they cleared a 30' x 30' patch and started planting vegetables, intent on growing their own food. Eventually, they figured, the garden would be situated just outside the kitchen. What the kitchen—not to mention the rest of the house—would ultimately look like hadn't been worked out yet. They knew only that they had $1,000 to put toward the house.

RESCUES

Onslow Ford lived in Mill Valley during this period but he kept a studio, a shared space with painter Jean Varda, on a ferryboat at Sausalito's Gate 5. Piled out in front of the boat was a stack of giant redwood timbers that had been part of the shipway's infra-

structure, where military vessels had been assembled during World War II. They were free for the taking. One day Onslow Ford rang up Blunk and tipped him off. "So J.B. bought a very early type of chain saw, his very first big, noisy tool like that," says Waite. "He had to use it and a blowtorch to get those timbers ready to be put onto a truck and hauled out of there. And they'd been charred, so he cleaned them up, chiseling out the worst parts. I wire-brushed a lot of them. And then we took the measurements and sat down with paper and pencil. We had a little bit of an idea of the basic design." The house was being realized in reverse, with the materials determining its design. This would be their process.

The heavy timbers from Onslow Ford ended up covering only a portion of Blunk's basic structural needs. The rest of the materials still had to be found. Nearby Ten Mile Beach at Point Reyes, often a gale-force-wind-groomed stretch of desolation, ended up serving as the couple's lumberyard. "This was just before the National Park [Service] took over that area," says Waite. "Most of the Point was private, ranch owned. With a little bit of chutzpah or contacts, though, you could drive out with a four-wheel drive to the beaches, and they were absolutely covered with driftwood. We went day after day after day, picking up these gorgeous milled 2 x 4s, 4 x 4s, and 4 x 6s, all oak, not terribly long—maybe 8 feet in average length. They probably came from a shipwreck. They were bleached white, some of them in perfect condition." All of them came at the right price.

The Ten Mile Beach driftwood score filled important gaps, allowing for the completion of the framing. For the exterior siding, Blunk scoured a local lumberyard and acquired a few truckloads of 1' x 12' red-

wood shiplap. But in what was one of the few actual materials purchases made for the house (at this time, redwood was plentiful and cheap), he took care to select only the silvery, sun-bleached boards at the tops of the lumberyard's stacks—the wood that didn't look new. For the front door, he combined two heavy, old-growth clear heart redwood planks, timber intended for a horse trough. "I remember the planks were very wide, thick, and so long they had to be delivered by

"My father was so connected to his place," says son Bruno Blunk, "and the work came from the place. He loved the house." Blunk had never built a house before, and he lived here until his death in 2002. ABOVE: The front elevation. Additions were built in the 1970s and '80s, but even then Blunk saved most of the windows for the sides and rear, which are open to the view. He didn't subscribe to Modern architecture's doctrine of transparency.

ABOVE: The view upon entering the house offers a
"material" wealth—a symphony of rich, soulful
patinas punctuated by unforgettable episodes of
landscape. Blunk had placed the tall window to perfectly frame a now-gone bay tree. The doorway at the
top of the stair goes to a master bedroom that was
added in 1985; the rest is original. Early on, after
Gordon Onslow Ford added a pale-green wash to the
interior woodwork of his nearby house, Blunk got the
idea to whitewash the ceiling boards. OPPOSITE: The
table, also original to the house's first incarnation, was designed by Waite. The stools are by Blunk.

a tractor trailer," Waite says. The uniformity of the
lumberyard wood translated to less time with a saw in
hand, less puzzle solving.

The windows came from Petaluma, California,
retailer Friedman Brothers. "They had used *everything*—
all kinds of stuff," says Waite. "Those windows had been

salvaged from an old schoolhouse. They were beautifully
framed; they just needed the hinging. They were different sizes, so that dictated how we placed them. Some
were leaded glass, and we used those in the loft." Given
the "make or break" role of windows in a building's
design, this acquisition was another triumph.

ZEN ARCHITECTURE

While living in Japan for two years, spending time
with master potters Rosanjin Kitaōji and Kaneshige
Toyo and woodblock printmaker Munakata Shik ,
Blunk had been exposed to *minka*, traditional Japanese timberframe farmhouses. Blunk's stay with
Noguchi took place in Kitaōji's 200-year-old *minka*
farmhouse in Kamakura—a city that is regarded as the
source of Zen influence in Japan. In Inverness, Blunk
naturally gravitated to the architecture and methods
of construction that he encountered in Japan—the
Zen approach.

The house was realized without any formal plans
or even a rough model. Instead, Blunk improvised
on-site, and he did most of the work himself. He
had some help from his father-in-law, however, as
Waite recalls. "After rereading some old letters of my
father's, and J.B.'s to him," she says, "I'm sure my
Dad helped with some early engineering—done long
distance mostly, by mail." And the dimensions of the
giant charred timbers would have imposed certain
parameters. But, otherwise, Blunk was free to handle
the house as he might a piece of sculpture.

By 1960, the house had a roof, walls, and a sub-
floor—far enough along, as far as Blunk was concerned,
for the family to move in. They'd been in Inverness for
nearly four years already, and during that time Waite

had given birth to two young sons, Bruno and Rufus. The four of them would now share a house that had, on the first floor, only one room containing a kitchen/dining/living area and a sleeping nook and, forced into the gable on the second, a 9' x 10' sleeping loft with a low ceiling. The bathroom was outside. It had a toilet and a cast-iron laundry tub that doubled as a sink and a bathtub. They used the tub "knees up, like the Japanese do," Waite says. It was raw and it was cramped but it was *theirs*. They didn't have to answer to a bank.

CONTINUATIONS
AND INTRODUCTIONS

In 1972, a decade after Blunk had begun sculpting in wood and following his breakthrough commissions for the University of Santa Cruz (*Santa Cruz* in '68) and the Oakland Museum of California (*The Planet* in '69), two men knocked at the door, looking to speak with him about the house: Art Boericke and Barry Shapiro, who were then in the process of writing and photographing their 1973 book *Handmade Houses: A Guide to the Woodbutcher's Art.* Christine Nielson, by this time Blunk's live-in partner (Waite and Blunk separated in '66) and soon to be the mother of his daughter, Mariah Nielson, welcomed them in. When they stepped inside the house, Nielson recalls, "J.B. was sitting nude, watching some news item on TV. It was very unusual for us to have it turned on at that time of day, and I don't remember the story that was engrossing him. But J.B. was sort of caught in his birthday suit, saying 'Hi.'" Considering that so much of this house's interest has to do with its constructional "nudity," Boericke and Shapiro had to have seen their first encounter there as oddly fitting. The house made the book.

LEGACIES

The decoration in the Blunk House today is more pared down than it was when Shapiro photographed it for *Handmade Houses*. The rugs and the layers of accumulated objects shown in those photos are mostly gone, and the paintings on the walls have changed. In the 1980s, Blunk had a bedroom added off the second-floor loft, and adjacent to the living area the floor plan was extended to incorporate what had been

an outdoor shower—changes that dramatically altered the exterior profile. But even a decade after his death in 2002, the soul of the house is still very much intact. It's still very much J.B.'s house. The art on the walls and the furnishings throughout, all part of the permanent collection established by Blunk's children, came from the artist's hands. His dinnerware remains, still kept on the shelving that he built into a wall in the dining area.

The house is home to an artist's residency program now, and Blunk's daughter, an architect by training, is its director. When the artists arrive for their

OPPOSITE AND ABOVE: When Blunk needed something for the house, whether pulls for a lamp or even a sink, he went out to his barn shop and crafted it. With the bathroom sink, as with so many of his creations, the tooling marks in the redwood were left to serve as ornamentation.

orientation, Nielson serves them lunch using the very cups and plates that she grew up with in the house. "My mother and father and I each had our own plate," she recalls, "made, of course, by J.B. I remember having my favorites. I liked having my favorite cup, my favorite plate. Each piece was a singular expression."

Blunk, an artist and designer, made everything the family needed. Says Neilson, "If I needed a bed or if we needed a stool or a bedside table or even a towel rack, he would make it. I didn't grow up in a home where we went out and bought those things. I think that's really unique, really special to have a father who could do that."

Back in the 1960s and '70s, Onslow Ford would often come around with his distinguished friends, proudly showing off what he'd enabled. Here was the house of a *true* artist. There was nothing bloated or excessive about it. It was just pure expression. Because Blunk's heirs have been unified in their aims to preserve his legacy, the same can be said about the house today.

BLUNK HOUSE AND STUDIO. Inverness, California. James Blaine "J.B." Blunk, architectural designer and builder. Nancy Waite, Christine Nielson, and Mariah Nielson, interior designers.

In 1964, when 28-year-old Deva Rajan set out to build his house, he did so with the intention of reviving the Arts and Crafts-era tradition of using a labor force of artists. THIS PAGE: Stairs climb the lush hillside past a series of decks to the third-floor formal entrance, which opens to the illuminated living room. OPPOSITE: Deva Rajan, sculptor/ master builder/winemaker, at home, 2010.

Deva Rajan & Family

c. 1964–74

LIKE WEEDS IN A GARDEN, four middle-aged men dressed in black suits stood amid the skyscraping redwood trees that bordered the bottom of Deva Rajan's driveway. While passing by the living room window of the cabin that the 28-year-old shared with his wife and their young son, Rajan had picked them out. Given all the fighting over land in Canyon since his move there four years earlier, he'd half expected their arrival. He had known it was inevitable, anyway. Now finally, in the spring of 1964, it appeared that it was his turn to deal with the authorities. Others had tried resisting them and in the process had lost their homes. Rajan had no way of knowing which way it would go for him, but he wasn't going to back down. It had only been a year since he'd pulled together the $5,000 to acquire the house and its acre. This was home, at last.

"I went down the driveway to meet these East Bay Municipal Utilities District guys and I had my firstborn in my arms. He was about 12 inches long at the time," says Rajan. "And I was talking with them and they said, 'You know you can't live here anymore, right? We're going to take away this road.'"

"I looked them in the eyes and said, 'Do you remember when you were my age? Do you remember when you were my age and you had a dream? How would you feel about it if someone threatened you and was about to take away that whole vision? You'd fight for it, wouldn't you? Well, that's where I am right now.'"

BACK TO THE EARTH AND INTO TURMOIL

Canyon, California, an off-the-map ravine overflowing with redwoods, live oak, bay, and madrones that had once been a Wild West logging hub and lumberjack camp, had by the 1950s become the crown-jewel holding of the East Bay Municipal Utilities District, the regional water company of Contra Costa County. The sparse community that had grown up around the water company's property shared the same watershed land, a major drinking-water source. By 1960, when Rajan took up in a rental in Canyon at the start of his

The workshop door, like the others here, is a Rajan design inspired by doors at 1812-era Fort Ross, in Sonoma County, California. Rajan cast the bronze handle, and blacksmith Daniel Dole forged the strap hinges. The two solid redwood planks that form the door are 3 inches thick.

they'd succeeded in downsizing the population from 500 to 150. With cash at the ready, county officials had aggressively acquired 66 Canyon houses, burning many of them before the ink had dried on the deal paperwork. The residents that hadn't given in to the financial pressuring, meanwhile, were subjected to frequent harassment. "To facilitate its land grabbing," wrote Sol Stern in an exposé in *Ramparts* magazine in November 1969, "East Bay MUD began a propaganda campaign claiming that Canyon's septic tanks were polluting the nearby creeks that ran into its reservoir—a charge that has never been substantiated by any independent investigation."

Eventually the controversy was settled in the courts, and many of the residents who'd survived still remained in Canyon, their sense of community stronger and more tightly knit. (When threatened by "the black suits," Rajan got them to back off by suggesting that he'd call in news-station camera crews.) Some, like the Rajans, continue to live in Canyon today. But back in the '60s, the fight over Canyon was such an ordeal that, in 1971, a book was published about it, *Canyon: The Story of the Last Rustic Community in Metropolitan America*, by John van der Zee. Moving on the advice of his philosophy professor from his undergraduate work at Los Angeles's Pomona College— "If you're going to UC Berkeley, you have to live in Canyon. It's a great place to live!"—Rajan had walked right into this political firestorm.

So, too, did many Bay Area back-to-the-landers. For them, Canyon's sparsely populated forests, a place where some houses are accessible only by narrow footpaths, looked like an easily reached oasis. A 20-minute drive, or hitchhike, could get you out of the tense city and into Canyon's laid-back tranquility.

graduate coursework in sculpture at the University of California, Berkeley, the water company was 10 years into a strong-armed campaign to rid the area of its residents. Backing them were overzealous county building inspectors and the sheriff. In that decade

Here was the place to live off the grid. Maybe you'd do it in a tree house of your own design and construction, or perhaps a dome, or even a shack made entirely of discarded windows. And for a while you might even pull it off on someone else's land. In the middle to late 1960s, if you wanted to build radically and live unconventionally, many young people in the area assumed you had a good chance of accomplishing it in Canyon. The problem was that county officials, not to mention the community's older residents, didn't see it the same way.

The day "the black suits" arrived at Rajan's property to hand him his "30-Day Notice to Vacate," in his yard he was hosting a few friends with those very same convention-defying ambitions. One was living in a van. Another was crashing in a tent cabin. Like Rajan, both men were highly educated and talented carpenters. Little did the officials know that the three friends were readying to build a monumental new house on that same site—a house built with the intent to last for the growing Rajan family.

CALLINGS

In 1963, after having completed his UC Berkeley master's program, Rajan was hired by the university to teach sculpture. He knew that it wasn't what he was supposed to be doing, however. Much earlier, his calling had found him. All through college and graduate school Rajan had worked as a construction laborer, an apprentice, and a journeyman. At the time, he thought he was just doing it for the money, to get through school. In fact, he'd fallen in love with it. After teaching one year, he decided to quit with the idea of building houses with artists. Canyon House, the

The redwood shakes, a defining feature of woodbutcher design and construction, lend the building a bark-like skin that weathers to become one with the forest.

new residence for his family, would be his first major effort in that direction and the inspired beginnings of his soon-to-be-founded company, Canyon Construction. It would end up being a handmade house on a scale seldom achieved.

WELLSPRINGS

Like so many houses made from salvage, Canyon House came together on paper only after the material was on hand to build it. But as quickly as the search was started, the sources emerged. Using their pickup trucks, Rajan and his friends cleared Oakland-based Ballinger Lumber's entire yard of reclaimed fir. "They gave it to us on the condition that we would haul *everything* away. We did that for days and days and days," he says, "until the whole place was empty." That wood was used in the roof construction. A slew of 12' x 12' redwood timbers, perfect for posts, were rescued from two downed Sacramento Northern Railway bridges. An out-of-commission Eureka railway trestle provided 8' x 18' fir timbers, which ended up as beams. "The 8' x 18' timbers were dirt cheap," says Rajan, "because they were too heavy to lift if you didn't have equipment. That was perfect for us because we had a crane."

Out of the old Hall of Justice in downtown San Francisco and headed for a landfill came 3' x 20' fir planks, material that was ideal for structural flooring. (To get the wood, they bribed the landfill's bulldozer operator with whiskey.) Tempered glass from a Bay Area window company was sourced without any price

tag. "In the process of tempering it, sometimes the glass sizes will change so that they can't be used," Rajan says. "And they throw all of that glass away. So we used to go down there and just get loads and loads of tempered glass, free." A La Honda, California, redwood that had been hit by lightning also contributed. "We got permission to drop this tree—you could walk inside it at the base, where it was burned—and from that, in two weeks, two of us split all the shakes for the house. We'd drive over there and come back every day with our trucks loaded." Another prized score was a gift of redwoods from a friend's 3,000-acre ranch in Fort Bragg. "We just cut trees the longest they could haul on the truck, which was 50 feet," Rajan recalls. "And that determined the height of the house."

INTERCHANGES

Although Rajan was a skilled artist and craftsman and, having an art-history education, was fluent in architectural history, he had never taken architectural design classes. However, coming from a construction background, he could read plans. By the time he was ready to create the basic design of the house, he'd taught himself how to draft. Meanwhile, he'd befriended a structural engineer who had taken a liking to his sculptural work. They worked out a deal whereby Rajan would get the necessary structural calculations in exchange for gifting the engineer one of his artworks. "And that's how we pulled permits," he says.

The permitted drawings contained the major brushstrokes of the finished building, but the intricacies of the overscaled post-and-beam architecture and the house's unique open feel crystallized once Rajan and the other builders had tools in their hands.

OPPOSITE: Spanning the 31-foot width of the living room are a series of 8" x 18" fir beams salvaged from a decommissioned railway trestle in Eureka, California. The wood-burning stove was originally an ocean buoy picked up from the Oakland naval supply yard for $5. Rajan enlisted Fritz Hagist to repurpose the buoy as a functional art object. (It took seven men to carry it up the hill and into the house.) The room's floor is black slate. The decor reflects the family's strong connection to India.

"Inspectors in those days were more concerned with electrical, plumbing, structural integrity, and stuff like that," he says. "There was a lot of latitude to improvise. We had no problem being very free with what we built. We began to just change things to create spaces that were interesting. Just by cantilevering beams farther out, you'd get a larger room." Much of the detailing was inspired by the hand-hewn, heavy-timber structures at Fort Ross, the Northern California Russian settlement built in the early 1800s.

Rajan designed his house to stand above the shadows of its wooded-ravine site and to make full use of a hillside, combining a 5,500-square-foot floor plan with 2,000 square feet of decks that cantilever, like outreaching arms, from each level and onto the slope. The activities of every floor in the four-bedroom, three-bath configuration can spill out effortlessly into the forest and toward the views. The project's scope was immense.

A DECADE IN THE MAKING

In 1974, 10 years after starting construction, enough of the house was completed for the family to move in. The rest of the needed work, Rajan reasoned, would come together eventually. That year, he wrote a poem, "My Half-Finished House," to commemorate the occasion, which included the lines: "This new life, this fine building.... / Far beyond the dreams of the Drafting table."

In 2011, when you visit the Rajans at Canyon House, you find a home that's grown along with the family that built it. In the nearly 40 years since the house was "ready," four Rajan children have been raised within it. In 1981, a new bedroom suite was added, and the tremendous skylit living room, origi-

nally designed to be open to the elements, was finally closed in with windows. In 2001, the house got an elevator, and all the tempered glass was replaced with custom double-glazed units. The kitchen, also recently renovated, no longer doubles as the living room.

But some things haven't changed. In his garage workshop, Rajan still crafts award-winning wines, just as he's done since 1964. Collaborating yet again with his Canyon neighbors, one of whom is the son of a carpenter friend who helped build Canyon House, Rajan has just finished blending a red and two whites. He lights up when discussing that work, just as he does when expressing his feelings about this house.

"While we were building and creating our homes in Canyon," Rajan adds, "I think that we were just swept away by the joy of building. It was the joy of finding materials and figuring out how to make them work; the joy of building without funds; and the joy of building things together. It was the joy of helping each other unconditionally."

CANYON HOUSE. Canyon, California. Deva Rajan, architectural designer and builder. Bruce Johnson, built-in furniture. Joan Machiz and Michael Lien, stained glass. Carpenters: Ethan Allen, Steve George, Gotosan, Ichikawasan, Jim Kirkwold, Michael Malott, Seth Melchert, Dean Pratt, Jeff Pratt, Dan Richards, Barry Smith, and Michael Westling.

Lloyd Kahn & Family

c. 1967—68

THE USUAL MORNING FOG BLANKET was gloriously pulled back this July 1967 day, treating the entire canyon to a continous simmer. In the absence of a tempering sea breeze, Boris and Filippa Veren and their guests, Bill and Barbara Spring, had made the long walk down the isolated property's steep gravel driveway to the creek-fed swimming pool, an unlikely oasis on the Verens' land that was openly situated in an ocean-view corridor, about 50 feet below a Highway 1 bridge. On the poolside table, a stack of bath towels shaded an open bottle of Chardonnay. The bathers' clothes, every last stitch of them, draped the chairs. As they drank the wine, swam, and cooled themselves into contentment, the Springs remarked to their

Before Lloyd Kahn influenced multiple generations as the *Whole Earth Catalog*'s shelter editor and an author/publisher of books on the same theme, he lived in Big Sur, where he created this house for himself and his family. Kahn built the home in a hurry, conceiving a simple shed-roof design that he could construct alone. THESE PAGES: The front elevation is an image that has gone mostly unchanged in 40 years, save for the life-size horses by current resident Barbara Spring, a sculptor who works in wood. OPPOSITE: Lloyd Kahn in the late 1960s, his Big Sur years.

friends on the utter sublimity of their spot in life. But then, suddenly, they saw a policeman on the bridge, standing outside his car and focusing a pair of binoculars aimed right at them. Moments later, Barbara remembers with a laugh, "He came down the road and said, 'You're under arrest.' He was a new policeman. We were in the nude, and he thought we were trespassers."

The Springs, Bill a businessman and Barbara a fast-rising sculptor, had been coming to Big Sur, as renters, since '52 and had had their share of unexpected run-ins but never like this. The tiny community's new designation as a rural outpost of the Haight-Ashbury hippie scene was forcing certain changes on it that, as was becoming increasingly evident, weren't sitting well with local law enforcement. The four friends, each then in his or her 50s, weren't hippies though; they'd simply gotten caught in the crossfire. As it turned out, a San Francisco lawyer, Tony Serra, had to be retained, and he cleared both parties of the charges. Serra had taken the case after having been introduced to the Verens in the process of handling a special deal on behalf of their friend and newly hired property caretaker, Lloyd Kahn.

An insurance agent and competent amateur builder from Mill Valley, California, Lloyd Kahn, in 1965 and at 31 years old, had hitchhiked across the

The dining and living areas. Once Spring settled in and began installing her wood sculpture, the house became irreversibly hers. In every room, the line between what's art and what's not is wittily blurred. The dresser, books, and vase with the window and partially drawn shade compose the sculpture *Playboy in Drawer*. The large hunk of meat on the cutting board (on the counter at right), *Well Done*, is also a Spring piece.

Bill and Barbara Spring in 1962, the year of Barbara's first one-man show at the Lucien Labaudt Art Gallery in San Francisco.

United States. By the time he'd returned home, he'd arrived at some revelatory personal conclusions. Principal among them was that he was done with the path he'd been on. Within a year, Kahn was on a different plane—standing on a construction site high atop a Pacific-facing Big Sur cliff, wearing Levi's and a pair of work boots, while alternately swinging a hammer and negotiating the placement of a series of 30-foot-long, half-ton reclaimed bridge timbers. He'd left his life in Mill Valley, not to mention the desk job, signing on as a carpenter of a George Brook-Kothlow–designed house for 400-acre Rancho Rico. A year would pass, during which he opted to live in the ranch's old chicken coops, before he was on the move again. The Veren property was the next landing pad. With a deal that allowed Kahn as caretaker to be a home-owning guest on the couple's acreage, he was set to build his own place in Big Sur, a house for himself, wife Sarah, and young son Peter. He'd come up with a design, and at a vista-rich location between the Verens' house and the pool he'd terraced a portion of the slope to make way for a foundation. Now he just needed to find the right materials.

"And so I started collecting," recalls Kahn. "The posts were 8" x 12" double-track railroad ties—redwood. The girders and the roof beams were 30-foot-long Douglas fir 2 x 14s that had been part of a horse stable in San Francisco. They came from the Cleveland Wrecking Company. I tore down a farm labor camp in Salinas for a lot of the materials. And then I split shakes in the woods around Palo Colorado [an area at the north end of Big Sur] using deadfall redwoods. You'd sometimes find old growth that's not long enough for somebody to mill, you know? So I did that. Sometimes, I'd go into the woods and cut up the tree, split it into bolts with wedges and a sledgehammer, and then bring it all back home and make the shakes at home using a froe and a bowling pin." Just as he'd done in 1963, the year his second and last Mill Valley house (a self-built John Stonum design, the merits of which got him the Rancho Rico project) was completed, Kahn intended the Big Sur home to comprise used parts and pieces. Likewise, he was handling the construction workload mostly alone. "The beams in the Big Sur house are sandwiched together, and I did those by myself," Kahn explains.

CONTEXTURE

What by necessity grew quickly on the canyon's hillside is a straightforward box, its shed roof canted in harmony with the slope of the site. Although Kahn admits that it wasn't his intention, the exterior's redwood shakes quote not only medieval architecture but also Big Sur's sense of place, its late-nineteenth-century ranch-architecture traditions as carried forth by the likes of Sam Trotter. The unconventionally placed reclaimed windows allude to the idiosyncrasies and strong independent spirit of the designer-builder. Throughout the design, uniformity was ardently avoided. In a certain sense, Kahn admits, the driving ideas behind the house's architecture and construction were a response to what he'd been working on that first year in Big Sur. "I'd just been involved in building a house out of very heavy big timbers, a huge, expensive house. . . . I wanted to do something simple and practical, and I knew how to do post and beam." With the design and construction of his house, Kahn was indeed reacting, but not overreacting. This building was right for its site and its users. It would end up becoming a classic Big Sur house.

PATHS AND BYWAYS

By the time he started the project, Kahn knew both Big Sur's landmark buildings and its well-hidden, steep-terrain, quirky shelters. He'd been to Nepenthe. He'd studied the free-form artistry and craftsmanship of the various shake-clad, heavy-timber-and-stone buildings that Doug Madsen built for his property. He'd seen the hand-hewn redwood houses of Sam Trotter. He'd also looked closely at Deetjen's. "When you go to a place that's got something, got some character and soul," Kahn says, "it just makes all the life that goes on inside that place different—and better. And Deetjen's is a perfect example of that." But he never consciously set out to riff on any of these buildings.

"I saw a lot of things," Kahn adds. "Back in Mill Valley, when I started building, I was interested in Frank Lloyd Wright and [Paolo] Soleri. And then I kind of gravitated toward Bernard Maybeck and Julia Morgan, these wonderful Bay Area architects. The Marin County style of redwood and small-paned windows and simple structures…. I mean, that's what we learned in the chicken coop—people and their architects go to such lengths to be clever. It seemed

At the rear of the house, a fixed ladder in a plywood-lined hallway reaches a bedroom that Kahn tucked into the cant of the roof. When the house was built, the electrical elements were left out in the open because it was the most practical option for dealing with the exposed structure. Nowadays the practice is part of a desired look.

to me, back then, that men looked at buildings from the outside and women looked at buildings from the inside." Here Kahn was siding with the women. His house wouldn't exert its seductive powers until after it had you inside—sheltered.

LUMINOSITY

The finished interior that the Kahns settled into in early 1968 was a showcase of gorgeous wood. Whereas the exterior indeed suggested little more than "a roof overhead," quiet and unassuming and always deferring to the natural surroundings, the inside of the house conveyed that rare quality that Kahn found in the Deetjen's structures. In the daytime, with all those windows placed both low and high on the walls, the interior's dark woods took on a vibrant, golden glow. "It was built to leave all the wood exposed," he says. "It's not snazzy or clever. It's just a very simple space with real, nice wood. That kind of warmth and quality makes you feel good." The interior proved invalid the tenet that natural wood finishes are gloomy without paint. Kahn had thrown that out the window along with practically every other late-1960s convention of design and construction.

FULL CIRCLES

In February of 2011, Barbara Spring, now 94 years old and a widely collected sculptor and still carving wood, is seated comfortably at the Kahn House's dining room table. It's a "nice, crude, big" piece of furniture that Lloyd made for the place in 1968. This is Spring's house and studio now. It's been this way since 1972, the year she and Bill, her now-deceased husband,

The crude kitchen Kahn built from old redwood railroad ties and Douglas fir planks, which had been part of a farm labor camp, represents everything our consumer culture teaches us to see as inadequate for the home. And yet Spring, with her artist's eye for detail and highly developed understanding of materials, preserves it, even as she's found considerable success as an artist. For 40 years, she's prepared meals here.

acquired it from the Verens for $13,500. By the summer of '69, Kahn began contributing to the *Whole Earth Catalog*, quickly taking on the prominent role of shelter editor. Kahn had also become a passionate advocate of Buckminster Fuller's geodesic domes. So much so, in fact, that in a few years, following a stint constructing domes for a Northern California alternative high school and the subsequent rapid-fire publication of his *Domebook 1* (1970) and *Domebook 2* (1971), Kahn found himself a figurehead of the international dome phenomenon that swept the early '70s. After concluding soon thereafter that domes were "wrong in almost every way," he would go on to write and photograph the landmark book *Shelter* (1973).

Spring vividly remembers thinking the house was too "Hansel and Gretel," but then they fell in love with it. In Barbara's hands for four decades now, the Kahn House remains much as it was when Lloyd, Sarah, and Peter closed the door to it for the last time in 1969. Spring has painted some of the interior woodwork, and she added on a room. Behind the house, on an octagonal slab where Kahn had built a dome, she added a small building that serves as her studio. But otherwise, the artist has cared for the place with a preservationist's zeal.

"I have changed things in this house to suit myself but I try not to alter Lloyd's ideas," Spring says.

"I think what it is about this house is, his freedom comes through me—his freedom with materials, his freedom in how he thinks. How I think in my work is how he thinks in his work. When I left art school, I had to get rid of most of the stuff I'd learned—the rigid stuff. I got knowledge from it but I had to get rid of it so I could get my own freedom. And in this house, Lloyd showed that freedom that I look forward to in my work. He doesn't inhibit me. In other houses, I don't feel that."

You wouldn't be able to pay a decorator to contrive what Kahn achieved instinctively in this house. In its patinas lives exuberance. When Spring hosted legendary architect and tastemaker Philip Johnson at the house, he was so taken by it that he promptly tried to persuade her to sell. "It has a feeling," the architect of the Glass House told her.

KAHN HOUSE. Big Sur, California. Lloyd Kahn, architectural designer and builder.

THESE PAGES: For Jeff Bishop and Kas, the dome they built on Big Sur's Partington Ridge was the killer riff to the song they never had time to complete; the call of other adventures got in the way. When the present owners, an artist and a carpenter, took over the house, they were able to improvise and fill it out. The projecting gabled wing at the front, an art studio that extends from the original dome (at the top of stairs to the right), was one of their best moves. Its reclaimed small-pane windows and Douglas fir shiplap stay true to Big Sur's vernacular. RIGHT: At the partially completed house in the early 1970s, a guest steps out and greets the day.

Kas & Jeff

c. 1971

THE BRANCHES AND LEAVES of the live oaks split the afternoon sunbeams into beautiful kaleidoscopic dapples. In this moody, flittering light, the stacks of old redwood railroad ties and the oxidized steel pipe and straps looked alive. Jonathan "Kas" Kasparian and Jeff Bishop had, since early morning, been working on building the dome that they'd designed. With a generator at their disposal, the two old friends, both 20-something and recently transplanted from London, were making fast progress. A stereo system had been wired in, and Crosby, Stills, Nash, and Young's *Déjà Vu* was booming. All day they had been soaking up the effects of a different sort of "sunshine," LSD, which brought a levitational dimension to the task at hand. But the feeling of floating, assisted as it was, wasn't a stretch of reality. After all, they were standing on scaffolding fixed to the side of a wildflower-covered mountain, at an elevation of about 2,000 feet,

and with an above-the-clouds view of the coast. Day after day, this is how they had worked.

As the sun began to set and the work was winding down, Kasparian and Bishop could hear drumming coming from up the hill. A young guy who called himself Rainbow, a neighbor, pulled up in his white Mercedes to say hello. He and his "adopted family" lived in a communal situation a little farther up the hill, on the historic Jaime de Angulo ranch. Musicians for the most part, the group of them had become known for their outdoor jam sessions. Rainbow was different, however. "Most of the time, he was stark bollock naked," Kasparian says. "He'd have a shirt on but nothing from the waist down." True to form, when he got out of the car he greeted them in the nude. It wasn't exactly out of step with the time and place. "There was

a whole scene going on up at the ranch then," says Kasparian. "There were all these hippies, people eking out an existence. They all lived on their wits, and they all had beautiful kids. One of them was called Forest. One of the mothers was called Storm, and her kid was called River. There was a guy called Mr. Natural. They were all sort of artisans in some way; they made jewelry or whatever. And they used to play fantastic music. The musicians called themselves Big Sur Light and Power. We would be at the dome and would hear the conga drums wafting across the canyon from deAngulo. People out of their heads on acid, dancing and things—it was a real scene, man." And it was the backdrop to a real shift in Big Sur's building scene, a move away from the tried-and-true pioneer ways and into a realm more expressive and often more creative.

LEFT: The front entrance. For the dome's ground floor, found redwood railroad ties were used as posts and beams and even as infill. OPPOSITE: The kitchens of Big Sur's older houses tend to be built of redwood left untouched, but this one belongs to a painter and lover of color. When the weather's right, during the preparation of dinner, the windows behind the redwood-slab counter get swung out toward the garden and the outdoor bed that sits in a field of wildflowers.

BEGINNINGS

By the time of the Dome's construction Kasparian had
been in Big Sur for less than two years. In 1969, upon
hearing of his impending plans to leave his native
London and go to San Francisco, a friend had urged
Kasparian to instead look up her father, archaeologist
Giles Healey, at his place on Big Sur's Partington
Ridge. When the 24-year-old carpenter showed up
at Healey's door, "two months after *Easy Rider* came
out," he received the kind of warmth that his friend
from back home had promised. He now had a place
to live in Big Sur (in Healey's 1937 redwood house
Mucha Vista, which had been built by Sam Trotter for
himself), something he'd known he'd wanted from the
moment he had set foot there.

Soon it became apparent that Healey's welcome
was turning into something more momentous than
what Kasparian had originally come for. In that first
year, the experience of Big Sur transformed the young
Londoner's life, both personally and in his work as a
designer-builder. "I had always dreamed that a place
like that existed," Kasparian says. "There were all
these incredible structures. The little cabins behind

The dome portion of the structure, the upper level, accommodates only the master bedroom. The rectangular ground floor was built large enough to fit not only the kitchen, but also a small living area with stove and a sleeping nook. In this intimate space, the artist and the carpenter raised their son. The little nook was his bedroom through his teenage years.

Deetjen's. . . . I'd never seen anything like Nepenthe, that sort of architecture. 'This is it!' I remember thinking. 'I can do what I want here. I can *build* whatever I want!'" Eventually, Kasparian would leave behind an important built legacy of his own in Big Sur.

Nine months after Kasparian's settling on Partington, his carpenter-friend Jeff Bishop was on his way from London to join him. Collaboratively, Kasparian and Bishop would go on to design and build a wide array of structures in the area, always with an eye toward using reclaimed materials and pushing the creative envelope. They did houses in both folk- and high-art styles. They were the builders of architect Mickey Muennig's 1976 "Owl House," an early project in nearby Carmel. They did barns. Their in-town work got them projects out of town, including Alice's Restaurant at Malibu Pier, a showcase of reclaimed wood, brass, and stained glass. Independently in Big Sur, Kasparian built much of the Michele Muennig House [see pp. 192–197] and parts of Mickey Muennig's Greenhouse [see pp. 186–191]. Kasparian would eventually relocate to Los Angeles for an extended period, where his solo work included the renovations of the Holiday House and Sunset, the restaurant. In the 1980s, he and Bishop ended up in Nicaragua as part of the volunteer building brigade APSNICA, with Bishop staying on there permanently. But back in the early 1970s, when they were beginning in Big Sur, what Kasparian and Bishop really wanted to do was to build domes. To get started, they took out an advertisement in the *CRADLE*, a local newspaper. "CRADLE stood for Coast Residents Association, Dead, Living, and Emerging," says Kasparian, laughing. "That was the '70s, man. We put an ad in there saying, 'Geodesic dome erections.'"

Domes weren't an easy sell, however. Although they would eventually get a few built in the area, they had to be their own first clients.

HOME SWEET DOME

The structure came together as a hub-system wood dome constructed of Douglas fir 2" x 4" struts, with the hubs made from 4-inch-wide steel pipe. A rectilinear box fashioned from the railroad ties and a variety of newly milled timber composed the geodesic's foundation, resulting in a two-story living space. Found tongue-and-groove Douglas fir sheathed the interior. The floor plan was simple: the dome itself contained a sleeping loft, while the ground-level rectangular volume allowed for a living area, a fireplace, and a kitchen. An outhouse was built nearby.

Built on a friend's property on Partington Ridge, a short walk from the house where Kasparian was living at the time, the Dome was to be a simple shelter for Bishop. In its ever-evolving state, though, the place would, over the years, alternately serve as home to both of its designer-builders, before ending up with its present owners. Bishop had originally put forth the idea for it, remembers Kasparian, after reading Lloyd Kahn's 1970 book *Domebook 1*. It was pure serendipity, then, or maybe fate, when, in early 1972, Kasparian and Bishop learned of a disassembled dome on a property on Big Sur's southern coast, available for the taking. When they arrived to claim the structure and load it into their truck, artist Barbara Spring greeted them and showed them where it was. Spring had just acquired Lloyd Kahn's old house (see pp. 96–103), and she was letting go of the *Whole Earth Catalog* shelter editor's now-dilapidated early geodesic effort to make

room for her studio. Big Sur Dome, as it was called, a dome featured in Kahn's *Domebook 2*, ended up serving as a greenhouse next to the dome house designed and built by Kasparian and Bishop. Their dome experience had, well, come full circle.

EXPERIENCED

In 2011, 40 years after they gave up London for Big Sur and started building together, Kasparian and Bishop, both of them now in their 60s, reconnected. The location was Kasparian's house in England, where since 1995 he's had his design, construction, and architectural-salvage business. Over dinner, the conversation landed on the subject of their old days on Partington Ridge and the dome. "Those were the best times of my life, living there and doing what we did," Bishop offered. Another record was put on the turntable, another log hit the fire, and two more shots of Cuervo Gold were sunk.

"Big Sur was pretty unique then," says Kasparian today. "In the late 1960s and early '70s, a hell of a lot of people came through there. Meeting Mickey Muennig was like a catalyst; since then, I don't think I've done a single project that doesn't have a curve or a radius somewhere. I've been told the bohemian style of Big Sur in the '60s and '70s influenced construction up and down the West Coast. It also influenced all the work that I did and continue to do. But when you're in the middle of something, you don't always realize it."

THE DOME. Big Sur, California. Jonathan "Kas" Kasparian and Jeff Bishop, architectural designers and builders.

Leslie Clark

c. 1971—73

BEFORE SHE FOUND ACCLAIM as a painter and opened her Ojai gallery, before she launched her Nomad Foundation to help the nomads of Niger, Africa, Leslie Clark was renting an old shack in Ojai's Topa Topa Mountains. The cabin had no electricity and no running water. Barely 20 years old, fresh out of a few years of college, and newly married to first husband Eric Little, she had aspirations of starting a commune. Ojai in the late 1960s and early '70s was a hippie settlement, and so within the burgeoning counterculture Clark and Little easily found enthusiastic participants for their experiment. They rehabilitated the shack and made it livable but before they could get the commune fully up and running the cabin's owner broke the news that he planned to sell. "So we decided we wanted to do our own place," recalls Clark. "My mother said it was okay to build on her property. We concluded we needed to have something that was just for us. Part of it was that we weren't really social. We were isolated, and we *loved* being isolated." The new house, it was resolved, would be designed by the then-aspiring artist. The couple would build it themselves.

CONNECTEDNESS

Cutting through the Clark family's ranch is a long, winding, and, at times, steep dirt road that eventually leads to a scenic plateau with an elevation of 2,800 feet. There, overlooking Lake Casitas, is where Leslie and Eric built their house. The site was one that Clark knew intimately. "As a kid, I'd ride my horses there," she says, "and I'd make tree houses there and things like that. I loved the place, because it has such a spectacular view." In 1971, with her design drawings finally past Ventura County's permit-process checkpoints, Clark and Little were ascending that familiar bumpy road in the farm's dump truck, hauling yet another precarious pile of timbers to their construction site. At one turn, because the payload was so excessive,

The Clark House is exceptional for how the builders' artistic vision encompassed every surface of every room. Since 1989, it's belonged to Lance and Sheila Smigel. OPPOSITE: The living room. When you enter the house, a series of spoked 6" x 10" reclaimed fir beams draws attention to the two-sided lava-rock fireplace, which is framed with sandblasted reclaimed fir 12 x 12s, each bolted with giant oxidized-steel straps. The oils are by J.J. Perry. BELOW: A 2010 Sheila Smigel drawing of her home. She calls the house Shangri-LaSh.

The 2,200-square-foot house sits on 40 acres, at an elevation of 2,800 feet. ABOVE: The front entrance maintains a certain inviting, hobbit-house kind of appeal, a charm that only becomes more seductive inside.

thing because we were so young. People that young often didn't have the money to have land. Fortunately, my family was willing to let me build on theirs." While the work was ongoing, Clark and Little lived in a small trailer that they'd parked right next to the site.

EXTEMPORANEOUS EXPRESSION

The couple had lucked into acquiring the heavy timbers that largely determined the overall design. They'd connected with Ventura-based carpenter and salvaged-wood collector Paul Chadwick, who took them under his wing and became their mentor on the project. When Chadwick discovered a soon-to-be-demolished citrus-packing structure in Fillmore, California, Clark and Little suddenly had their framing timbers—Douglas fir 12 x 12s. "They were all funky and whitewashed and stuff but it was fabulous wood," says Clark. "We cleaned it up and sandblasted it." Chadwick also came through with the trees used to make the free-edge planks that clad the exterior's upper story. The stone was likewise reclaimed, having been collected from the ranch itself.

But it was the interior that received most of Clark's creativity and the efforts of those that helped with the execution. Using a sandblaster and custom stencils, they ornamented the clerestory windows. The outsized ornamental steel strap hinges that hold the posts and beams came from old water tanks and were cut according to patterns she created on-site. For the floors, they collected scraps from the lumber-yard to make end-grain blocks and laid them out like bricks. She conceived the timber spiral stair—"I had to draw about three pages of plans for that thing." And she put the structural heavy beams to use as

the truck's wheels lifted a few feet off the road. "The truck just kind of bounced back down to the ground," Clark says, laughing. For her, the mishap stands out as symbolic of so much of the process of getting the house built: There were times when they lost traction. But the wheels always eventually met the ground again, and when they did the couple pushed forward. "It was really a process, and it was kind of an extraordinary

yet another eye-catching feature, a design that has them radiating out from two sides of the massive dual fireplace that breaks up the dining and living areas. "I liked the idea of the fireplace being the heart of it," Clark says. "I was just dreaming. I didn't do any engineering. I just thought it was a good concept." In 1973, they moved in, although it would be another two years before the house was considered finished.

REDIRECTING

By 1988, Clark was ready for a new challenge. In the intervening years, her journey had taken a number of significant turns. Although the house had served them well—"I loved that house, I still love that house," she says—Clark and Little had divorced. "I came up with an arrangement so that I bought him out of the

ABOVE, LEFT: As in the dining room, the living room was given clerestory windows—another example of "taking the long way home." For Clark, the feature was as much an opportunity for creative intervention as it was a constructional challenge. To create the etchings, she covered the panels with masking tape, drew and cut a stencil, then hit them with the sandblaster they'd borrowed for using on the salvaged timbers.
ABOVE: Smigel on the spiral stair, 2010. When Clark and her friends first laid the wood-block floor, they'd forgotten to let the blocks age before they glued them into place and sanded the surface. Within a year there was chipping and separation, so they redid the entire floor.

house." In 1980, while gaining her master's degree in fine art, she met Michael Price—the man whom she would later marry. Her art was also finding its way. For the painter and self-trained architectural designer, it was time. She and Price added a guesthouse and, soon thereafter, they put the home on the market.

In early 1989, a realtor was touring the house and walking a stretch of its 40-acre property with Lance Smigel, a real estate investor and a cofounder of CaesarStone USA, and his writer-artist wife, Sheila. The Los Angeles–based Smigels were seeking a weekend place. "When I first saw it, I felt instantly that I was in *The Sound of Music*," Sheila recalls. "I walked in and it was like, 'Yeah, this is what I always wanted.'" They acquired it that September.

Despite their original intentions of using the house for weekends only, the Smigels ended up making it their primary residence, only six months after taking possession. "After I moved in, I didn't really leave for about two and a half years," says Sheila, "other than to go to the grocery store and to the cleaners. It was such a big sigh of relief to leave L.A. and all that madness. I loved the house, and I still do. There's always something new to see. And that still holds true 21 and a half years later. It's always an adventure."

ONE OF A KIND

Among nature's greatest giveaways is an Ojai sunset. (Because of the valley's orientation to the east-west mountain range, Ojai is one of the few places in the world where you can experience a "pink moment"— the striking effect of the sun's reflection on the bluffs to the east.) And this property has one of the more advantageous stages for taking it in. The sunset on September 2, 2009, was unusually spectacular, however, and the timing was perfect. That evening, a group of intimate friends were gathered at the Smigels to pay farewell to Lance, who had recently died. As the sun began to fade away, everyone raised a glass and joined together in singing "For He's a Jolly Good Fellow." And then, "as soon as the sun went down," says Sheila, "a full moon came up on the opposite side. It was like everybody knew that Lance had come back for an encore. It was just too good."

CONTINUATIONS

Today, Sheila is directing the restoration of the house, intent on returning it to its "original glory." Just before dark, she'll swing open the French doors of her dining room, walk out onto her patio with a glass of wine, and cast her gaze across the valley toward a glow that never gets old.

CLARK HOUSE/SHANGRI-LASH. Ojai, California. Leslie Clark, architectural designer. Leslie Clark, Eric Little, and Michael Price, builders.

Mike & Mary Breen

c. 1984

AT JADE COVE BEACH, the rock- and gem-collector's wonderland on Big Sur's southern coast, Mike Breen always got lucky. Whenever he made his exit, climbing the steep trail that leads from the shoreline up and out to the parking area, he carried a loaded backpack and had an ear-to-ear smile. "He was such a rock hound," says his wife, Mary. "During the winter, when storms would cause rocks to fall from the mountains onto Highway 1, Mike would always say that he needed to run out and collect. Right after work, he'd be there. Among locals, he was known for it. He'd be on the side of the road somewhere, lifting the stones into his truck, and neighbors would drive by and rib him: 'Hey, Mr. Mike, those are my rocks!' But he always got there first, to get the good ones." Later, those finds—like the redwood slabs and so many other materials—would be painstakingly carried up to his hillside house. More often than not, they

THESE PAGES: The front elevation of Mike Breen's five-unit, redwood wine-barrel house—what's surely the most ingenious example of its kind anywhere. The tank on the right, an addition, is actually two tanks conjoined; the dome-roof center tank, Breen's original house, has a smaller tank behind it that holds the bathroom; and the tallest volume, also an addition, is a single tank that rises to three stories with help from a 5-foot, shed-roofed height extension. LEFT: Breen in the late 1980s, masterminding the entrance and the living room expansions. On what was his first major project as a builder, he worked mostly solo.

In the original volume, Breen cut a large opening in the tank's
2¾" x 5" staves and built on the bay that holds the kitchen. The
opening to the adjacent "entrance tank" was added the same way,
with a "that looks pretty cool" pencil line and a reciprocating
saw. The breakfast bar and stair-tread slabs were found materials,
mostly redwood. The stair accesses the sky-lit master bedroom.

became part of the mise-en-scène. The ever-resourceful Breen was a master at repurposing. The house he began building in 1984 is his shrine.

EUREKA

One day in September of 1982, Breen was on unfamiliar ground, struggling to maneuver his Winnebago up one of Big Sur's notoriously steep and narrow residential driveways. When he finally reached the top, he placed the vehicle in park for good. His native Michigan was now squarely in his rearview mirror. This was home. Artist Gregory Hawthorne, Breen's close friend and employer of the last decade, had just made the same cross-country transition, and he had brought his trusted assistant with him to continue their fast-growing endeavors at his new West Coast base. "Mike didn't like Lansing that much," Hawthorne says, alluding tongue in cheek to the midwestern city's often-punishing cold weather. "He was excited to move to California. Before he left home he'd bought a motor home, and he says to me, 'That's where I'm going to live when I get to Big Sur.'"

Parked next to Hawthorne's cabin, Breen rode out nearly 18 months in the camper. All the while, Hawthorne had been suggesting that he build a caretaker's house on his property. Finally, Breen grabbed a machete and took on the poison oak and brush that had a stranglehold on everything below the cypress trees on Hawthorne's hillside land. When Breen emerged, cuts and bruises and all, he walked into the artist's studio and announced to his boss that he'd found the perfect spot.

"I think I'm going to build a wine-barrel house," Breen told Hawthorne a short time after they agreed on the site. "And I said, 'what the hell are you talking about?'" Hawthorne recalls. "So he showed me some pictures of one he had seen. And then we went to visit a wine-barrel house, a rather simple structure that somebody had built in the backwoods. And I remember looking at him and saying, 'Are you nuts?' And he said, 'No, this is going to be cool.'" He'd never built a house. In fact, says, Hawthorne, Breen wasn't really even a carpenter.

BLENDING

By the late 1970s, wine-tank conversions for residential use, especially tanks made of redwood, had become popular among the more adventurous of the West Coast's back-to-the-landers. The Endangered Species Act of 1973 had made it challenging, if not impossible, for wineries to continue with their manufacture. The redwood tank wood was old-growth clear heart—the finest of all grades, free of imperfections. Suddenly the tanks, which often stood 18 feet tall and were 24 feet in diameter, were cheap and readily available to builders. Around the state, salvage yards were snapping them up.

The cooperage that Breen needed was found quickly, right in Big Sur. He chose two tanks, a red and a white, both of them tapered and made of redwood, that had been acquired from a winery in Napa Valley. For what would have cost between $10,000 and $20,000 today for each, Breen paid a total of $2,000. Getting the tanks back to the Hawthorne property, however, wasn't so simple a task. It required the kind of ingenuity and determination that then-32-year-old Breen was known for. Before they were disassembled and loaded onto a truck, each intensely perfumed 3" x 6" stave was numbered, like a puzzle piece, to ensure a precise

reconstruction. Once they were at Hawthorne's, the staves were carried by hand, board by board, from the driveway down a steep forest trail to the building site. Breen then hand-planed and oiled the interior side of each stave, to remove the grape pigment, crystallization, and other common residue and to seal it. "He wanted to keep some of the grape perfume in the wood," says Hawthorne, so each stave's exterior side was left untouched.

The original house's two-tank configuration accommodated certain practical needs: the bathroom, which went in the small tank, would be a separate yet interconnected part of the floor plan, which meant he wouldn't have to have an outhouse. Breen placed the structure out of sight, behind the profile of the large container, and used a reciprocating saw to cut the passage holes between the back-to-back structures. The larger volume was designed to accommodate two levels, with a small eat-in kitchen and living area on the ground floor and, upstairs, a very compact bedroom. Although he was in a hurry to make it all livable, doing the work both in the early mornings before his day job and on weekends, the builder still took extraordinary care with the detailing. A curvilinear stair with free-edge redwood-slab treads traces a wall in the large tank, providing a

seemingly floating, space-maximizing link between the two levels. With help from Micah Curtis's local metal shop, Breen designed and fabricated the stair's wrought-iron brackets himself. On that small second level, over the bed, he built a full-diameter skylight—similar to the glass roof of Mickey Muennig's dome [see pp. 186–191]. It opened up the space. "He was a real moon and star person," his wife recalls.

RECOGNITIONS

It was 1988 when Mary entered Mike's life, and soon thereafter he was adding three more tanks onto the house. The house now had formal and informal living rooms, a guest room, an office, and other devoted spaces. The original diminutive kitchen grew with the construction of a projecting bay, and to keep it consistent Breen built the façade using similar redwood tank stock. "When I came along," Mary recalls, "I looked at the tiny kitchen and then looked at Mike and said, 'You know I like to cook, right?'"

Just as he'd done in the original design, for every addition the amateur builder invented striking architectural features. Each detail was idiosyncratic, as Breen himself had crafted it. Inside, he designed and installed a variety of custom furniture, including built-in desks, sofas, and shelving. He also made the counter-tops, the breakfast bar, and details like door handles and latches. Outside, he built decks for each level and appropriated his rock collection for the foundation and the landscaping. All of it was artfully rendered. By the late 1990s, the house was becoming a

local showpiece; word was getting out. "All kinds of architects and artists and entrepreneurs came over. They all wanted to see the house that Mike built," says Hawthorne. "I was thrilled for him. It had become a part of the vernacular of the area. Mike wanted to make one of the coolest little handmade houses, not only in all of Big Sur," Hawthorne elaborates, "but in all of the country. He wanted to have his own little special spot."

BEARINGS

On May 4, 2008, Breen suffered a massive stroke and a brain aneurysm and died; his friends and colleagues agree that he wouldn't have been happy if he'd been forced to live an inactive life. Says Hawthorne, "The way he lived, it would've been horrible. He left this planet the same way he came in, with a bang."

Today, March 29, 2011, Mary is busy in the kitchen that her late husband made especially for her, putting the final touches on a Mr. Mike Lemon Meringue Pie, something she prepares and donates every year to the Big Sur Volunteer Fire Brigade. It's one of the ways, she says, in which she helps keep the memory of Mike Breen alive. "There's never been a time when I've taken this for granted," she says, tearing up. "I know what I have, and I appreciate it on a daily basis." The anniversary of her husband's death is on the horizon, and as she looks around the house she can't help but see him.

> BREEN HOUSE. Big Sur, California. Michael "Mr. Mike" Breen, architectural designer, builder, and interior designer.

OPPOSITE: For the living room, Breen crafted a built-in sofa and a low table using wood that would have otherwise gone to waste. On the mantel is a fragment of a whale's vertebrae that he found on a nearby beach. More Gregory Hawthorne paintings hang from the walls. ABOVE: The amateur builder thoughtfully staggered and sized the bathroom windows in line with the hillside view. Like most of the house's doors, the tub is partly constructed using leftover tank staves.

After his 14' x 14' tent
cabin burned, Scott Newkirk
(seated in window) designed
a new off-the-grid summer
retreat, a "handmade mod-
ernist bungalow." Utilizing
the only level surface on
the property, the surviv-
ing deck, he had the house
built with old barn wood.
The outcome ushers the
1960s and early '70s New
York woodbutcher tradition
into the new millennium,
retaining all the soul
while substantially raising
the flair.

Scott Newkirk

c. 2004

RIGHT THIS MOMENT, beneath a canopy of branches somewhere in the wooded world, a group of kids is clearing a spot on the forest floor and learning to drive nails into 2 x 4s and plywood, piecing together a hideout of their very own. Forty-something Brooklyn transplant Scott Newkirk remembers well such architectural adventures from his childhood in Mississippi. Nowadays, in summer months, when he makes his escape from the city to a peaceful scene along the Delaware River in Sullivan County, New York, he lands at an adult version. Situated on a hillside clearing of his hemlock- and fern-covered 50 acres, at the end of a long and bumpy dirt road, Newkirk's getaway is deliberately without electricity and plumbing. With the nearest metropolis hours away, the typical day's noise is limited to little more than birds chirping, leaves rustling, and the nearby brook rushing over its winding, stony bed. Here, grand simplicity is achieved—all in 300 square feet.

TIME AND SPACE

The house started with a fire and an old book. In 1998, Newkirk, an interior designer and a fashion stylist who's worked with the likes of Coach, John Varvatos, Calvin Klein, and Ralph Lauren, was browsing a used bookstore near

The degree of transparency Newkirk was
after for the brook-facing side of the house
(the loft panes are 4' x 6¾') gave him two
options: either find a classic Modern house
in demolition or go new. He ended up buying
standard aluminum-framed windows but
concealed the frames behind barn wood to
keep the character of the house intact.

Peconic, New York, where he was a regular weekender. There he stumbled upon a 1973 copy of Art Boericke and Barry Shapiro's *Handmade Houses: A Guide to the Woodbutcher's Art*. The book ended up in his home library, where it would remain, untouched, for the next five years. By the summer of 2000, Newkirk had exchanged Peconic for Sullivan County as his city-escape destination, and the following spring he and his father built a wood-framed tent cabin on his new acreage. "This all happened pretty fast," he says, "and the house I had in my head for the property was still only in my head. I needed a structure more immediately, to hang my hat, so I could begin to get to know the land. The tent reeked of the strange pioneer spirit that had begun to develop in me." Two joyful years of use ensued and then, while Newkirk was away, the tent cabin caught fire and burned to the base.

In the immediate aftermath of the fire, once back home at his New York City apartment, Newkirk was finally compelled to pull *Handmade Houses* back off the shelf. "Getting myself together," writes Sim Van der Ryn in the book's foreword, "started with getting my time and space into one place, with creating the possibility and essential conditions for that wholeness." For Newkirk, there was resonance in both what the book had to say and in its "ramshackle but always inspired houses built with found, collected, and reconsidered materials." It got his creativity percolating. Within two weeks of the fire, he had sketched out his own handmade house.

INQUIRY

The Sullivan County context that the stylist and designer stepped into when he acquired his land is one that's without distinct architectural traditions. Thus, when conceiving his house, after having given careful consideration to the area's history, he concluded he could start with a clean slate. "There are no historic homes around, no picturesque towns, no antique shops or charming restaurants," Newkirk explains. "Unlike the quaint hamlets of the Hudson Valley region, this area looks as if the people have always struggled to get by. But what the area lacks in social contributions, it makes up for in natural geographic beauty."

The absence of a vernacular freed his imagination. There were a few givens, however. He knew he would design the place to fit the platform that reached out from the hillside, the caisson-supported wood structure that had once afforded the tent its great vantage point above the brook (and that had survived the fire). He'd also determined that the house's interiors would have an effortless connection with the site. "One of my favorite architects and, in turn, one of my favorite houses is Rudolph Schindler and his King's Road house, built in 1922," Newkirk says. "What was important for me to borrow from that distinct structure was the relationship—the union—between indoor and outdoor space. And because my house would serve primarily as a summer retreat, this concept was realistic for a building nestled in the woods of upstate New York."

Fully embracing the low-tech, back-to-the-land lifestyle that the house affords him, if only on weekends and vacations, Newkirk happily steps outside and back in time in order to do the dishes. The water is brought in by hand, as the house is without plumbing. The simple windows here were crafted for the house.

An exposed structure
made of reclaimed wood,
especially old, notched
hand-hewn barn timbers
like those of the
living area/kitchen,
offers depth of charac-
ter—a storied richness—
that begs for minimal
decorative intrusion.
A fashion stylist and
interior designer,
Newkirk had many tricks
at his disposal, but
still he brought a light
hand to the task with an
anonymous earth-toned
Cubist painting; some
vintage black-and-white
photographs; "natural
oddities" and found
objects; and rustic
Modern furniture, all
placed to highlight
what's immovable. The
counter was made from
leftover barn wood.
The stair accesses the
loft bedroom.

AMERICANA

When you walk the path that leads through the trees and toward the house's stepped fieldstone entranceway, the profile of a simple, two-story, 14' x 14' box with a shed roof reveals itself. If you weren't already aware of the home's brief lifespan, you might mistake the board-and-batten structure as historical. It could easily pass for a nineteenth-century farm building, albeit one outfitted with new openings. This was Newkirk's intention. "By choosing to work with this reclaimed barn wood," he says, "I knew I would be able to create an immediate history, and I could have the framework itself be a design feature, with no effort. Sustainability was really secondary."

While shopping at a local farmer's market Newkirk had connected with Hall Smyth of Lumberland Post & Beam, an outfit that specializes in sourcing reclaimed materials. "He was showing reclaimed barn wood as an alternative idea to new wood flooring," says Newkirk. "We discussed my house idea and realized that he could provide all of the timber I would need. I never even priced out new wood or any alternative building material after this." The metal roof is likewise recycled, having once covered an old local restaurant. The whole aesthetic is so deeply ingrained in the American past that it wouldn't be inappropriate for any country setting. Here, it sings.

CURATION

Working with reclaimed wood is not the same as newly milled lumber. The imperfections in the timber can be especially demanding. A builder must have the hands for it. Perhaps because of the isolated location, Newkirk

didn't have an easy time getting his 300-square-foot house crafted. What he thought would be a three- or four-month job actually required three years. In the process, he went through as many builders.

The interior of the post-and-beam structure is all about economizing within its small footprint. On the first floor is the living area and kitchen; on the second is a small loft. But the relationship to the deck is so intimate, made possible by sliding doors, that the building envelope can easily be made to feel much more substantial. Custom windows, both fixed and operable, are atypically positioned on the wall to better capture the best vistas as well as light and breezes. Against the weathered backdrop of the old-wood walls, ceiling, and floor, Newkirk installed furnishings that harmonize with the exposed structural timberwork and avoid overwhelming the space. "Due to the fact that the house is not insulated," he says, "upholstery, with the exception of a few cushions, was not really an option. So in keeping with the theme established, I acquired several furniture pieces from my friend Jason Lamberth, who works in reclaimed exotic woods from Indonesia." These include the living area's free-form teak sofa bench and circular stool and, in the open loft area, a long bench that serves double duty as a bookshelf and a safety rail. The loft's bed is actually a wood-and-canvas camp cot topped with a mattress that Newkirk had specially made.

OPPOSITE: While the 6½' x 14' loft with its trapdoor, limited headspace, and bed fashioned from a custom mattress placed atop an old canvas camp cot has charm, mystery, and coziness to spare, for its designer the space is really about its connection to the outdoors. Newkirk likes being able to wake feeling as though he's in his own private forest, and a big part of that is healthy airflow; hence, the operable windows at each end of the room. Later in the day, he might light a candle, open the pivot door, and sit in the egg chair with a good book.

PAUSES

At the conclusion of each day here, now seven years after spending his first night in the place, Newkirk still climbs the steps to his sleeping loft with a certain contentment and peace of mind. He's still enthralled with it, with the outcome of his design and with the special connection to nature that it affords him. "Time here is different," he stresses. "You wake as the woods awakes. Or at least you are aware of the woods awakening. It starts with a single chirp of a bird, which gradually grows as his neighbors follow suit. Then the day begins to break, casting beams of light through the trees and into the house. You become aware again of the running brook, and at this point you make a decision: 'Do I wake now and witness this as it's happening, or do I just lie here, eyes closed, and drift in and out of sleepy consciousness?' The latter usually prevails."

NEWKIRK HOUSE. Yulan, New York. Scott Newkirk, architectural and interior design. Craig Petrasek, builder.

Not a Home but a Happening

The business of the innovator is to innovate, and Dave Sellers was not about to shake up the architectural establishment by designing an old family homestead. His ski house is for swingers—of the Tarzan sort as well as the social. It is not for people with physical disabilities or addiction to alcohol. This is one of the few houses in the world that it is possible to fall off without going outside.

The idea of the house is to take the weekend skier and put him not just out on a scenic mountainside but right in the treetops to enjoy a view undefiled even by his own driveway. Sellers achieved this by pinning his house to the hillside a bit below

the service road he and Bill Rienecke had pushed out across the north slope of a ridge of Prickly Mountain and making its main entrance—on the back, or uphill, side of the house—accessible by a bridge from the spruce-fringed driveway.

The visitor ducks into a tunnel through the drifts at the bases of the snow-steeped spruces, and walks across the 100-foot-long wood bridge—through whose floor the trunks of several trees pass. He enters the ski house at mid-level, to discover that the far side is virtually all windows, of many shapes and sizes, set in the walls of rooms and cubicles

at many levels and connect more or less, by stairs, ladd or other climbing aids. All windows hang high above cone clustered tops of the spru —and beyond that is the sp tacle—miles of snow-filled va and snow-draped mounta with Mount Mansfield, Vermon kingpin, on the horizon.

This obsession with the view the first, and just about the l way in which this house res bles other ski houses with th deep-cushioned dozing-pla smack up against big firepla and one huge picture wind This house is to the traditio chalet-style lodge as a Rausche berg is to a Turner landscape. is not a home; it's a Happeni

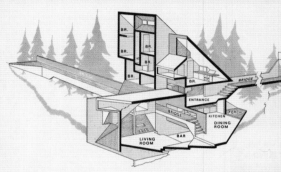

The many levels of the Bridge House can be observed in this cutaway drawing, shown in different shades to make the complicated design more legible. The 100-foot-long entrance bridge comes in from the rear (right). A second bridge, 65 feet long, runs out from the kitchen to a hillside rock which is used for barbecuing and sun-bathing. The house has just three footings: one each where the two bridges enter it and one beneath the bar. The

living room has an odd conformation and a wall that slants backward at a 15-degree angle. Niches notched into the wall serve as seats. Sellers sliced off all living-room corners and set large windows across the resulting angles. The pyramidal protuberance houses the built-in Mustang seats. In the bedroom section, the tall, narrow space is a kind of stairwell—a climbing chute in which are set steps, ladders and assorted climbing aids,

CONTINUED

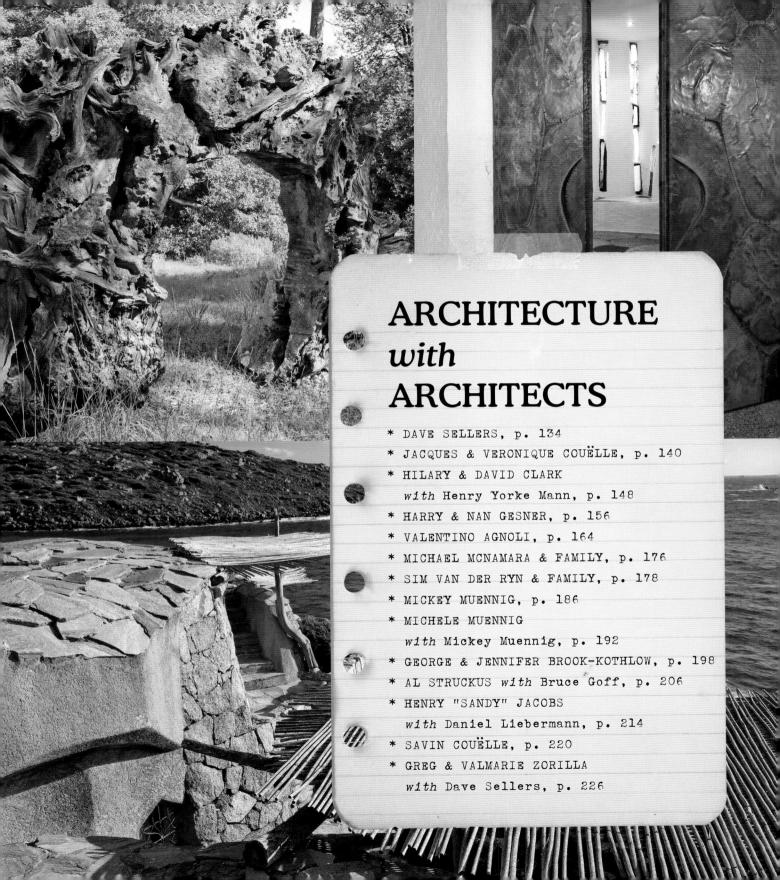

ARCHITECTURE
with
ARCHITECTS

Dave Sellers

c. 1966

ANOTHER LUNCH-HOUR touch-football game was coming to a close at 4 Potato Road on Prickly Mountain. As was customary, members of both teams, all of them recent architecture- and art-school graduates, subsequently congregated for a bit to talk shop. Just as they did at play, this group of friends also worked in teams, and dialoguing through design-and-construction issues had become an aspect of these midday breaks. On this particular sunny afternoon in the spring of 1966, 27-year-old Dave Sellers and William Rienecke, both of them budding architect-builders and title holders of the Mad River

In 1965–66, the door to improvisational architecture in America was made from scrap 2 x 4s and attached to a rural Vermont building called Bridge House. THESE PAGES: Dave Sellers ascends the climbing wall in his living room. The element of surprise doesn't come at the expense of normal household functionality but is part of it. LEFT: Sellers, architect/builder/engineer/plumber/electrician/entrepreneur, 1973.

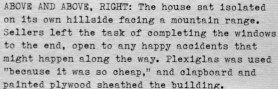

ABOVE AND ABOVE, RIGHT: The house sat isolated on its own hillside facing a mountain range. Sellers left the task of completing the windows to the end, open to any happy accidents that might happen along the way. Plexiglas was used "because it was so cheap," and clapboard and painted plywood sheathed the building.

Valley, Vermont, property they were playing on, had a couple of houses going up in their year-old experimental community, a place without building codes. One of them was taking shape as the ultimate skier's party pad, a 10-level house where every room offered postcard views. Its chief designer, Sellers, was also its builder, and he had taken to calling the project Bridge House. Having recently completed the seminal Tack

House just up the road, a residence of his own that almost immediately found coverage in the *New York Times*, the new project was Sellers's bold speculative venture. But this would be no ordinary spec house.

GROUNDWORK

Later that afternoon at the Bridge House site, an unnervingly steep spruce-covered slope with a dead-on view of Mount Mansfield's 4,395-foot-high peak, Sellers—skill saw in hand—was completing the plywood box beams of the two bridges that would anchor the house to the landscape and intersect in the living room. One of those structures was 100 feet long; the other was 65 feet. His friend John Lucas, on temporary leave from Louis Kahn's architecture practice, was helping him. Meanwhile, Edwin Owre was gluing together a stack of 2 x 4s that, when attached to some "welded-up springs for hinges," would become doors for Bridge House. One of Sellers's old buddies from Yale and a noted sculptor, Owre had been recruited early on to lend to the creation of the first few houses for Prickly Mountain and had become Sellers's chief collaborator. "I had a studio in New York after I got out of the program at Yale," recalls Owre, "and I was making some things down there. Dave called me up and said, 'Why don't you come to Vermont and we'll do some houses that have to do with artists and architects working together, to see what effect that has.'"

In the wake of Tack House's completion, Owre, then in his late 30s, was so thoroughly jazzed by the creative energy of the Prickly experience that sticking around for the next project was a given. "It was all about discovery," Owre says, "and trying to do with less and trying to get as much out of the materials and tools as we could." With Tack House, architect and artist had carved out their very own approach to the process of realizing a building. A rough cardboard model would be made at the start and would serve as "something of a reference point." But beyond that, it was all about free-form improvisation—step onto the building site and let the creativity flow.

There weren't any blueprints, nor were there any contractors or subcontractors around to bring their personal interpretations to the architect's vision. Practically every aspect of the house's design came together on the spot as the team went along. "When we'd talk about something, it would always be about the things that hadn't happened yet," says Sellers. "Because it was so exciting. It became a puzzle dealing with those unknowns." And the architects and artists did all the constructing and crafting themselves. "Several times," Sellers adds, "when stymied on a decision, we decided to build the best idea full-scale and evaluate it. Like stage sets, we then could move the parts around until it seemed like the best way to go, and then we would fix it. The term 'nail it' became the watch word when all was right." Many of the building materials they chose had once belonged to other structures. Many of the parts were conceived and crafted on-site, as the need for them arose. "Dave never liked to buy hardware," says Owre. "He'd rather make it himself or have it not be necessary." In short, the architects and artists of Prickly Mountain, most of them bringing design training of the highest order, had started their careers by turning their backs on the very industry for which they'd been groomed. With Bridge House, their most ambitious undertaking yet, the improvisatory approach was taken to its apex.

GUIDANCE

Before Sellers and fellow Yale Architecture alum William Rienecke acquired the 450-acre tract near the Sugarbush ski resort and formulated their pioneering design-build concept, Sellers had spent considerable time with Yale art instructor Robert Engman. A sculptor and Josef Albers protégé, Engman quickly became a major influence, introducing Sellers to, among other things, the philosophical teachings of Johann Wolfgang von Goethe. "Bob would quote Goethe," Sellers recalls, "who said, 'If you can't make a decision immediately, don't try. Because if you do, you'll probably do it wrong. Go to the periphery, where you know what you have to get done, and then work your way toward the problem situation.' " This is how Bridge House was realized.

GRATIFICATION

The sun was beaming out from behind Mount Mansfield's shoulder and everything else was whitened—blanketed in snow. A year had passed, and Bridge House was finally finished. *Life* magazine was inside taking photographs for an upcoming "Ideas in Houses" feature, the entire Prickly Mountain gang, their dogs, and even the local pet goat in attendance. *Life*'s photographer was staging a partylike atmosphere, and this group didn't have to try hard to get there. In fact, the house made such a vibe mandatory. Most of the activity was happening in the double-height, red-yellow-blue-green living room. The space openly embraced the sky and the valley below through large Plexiglas windows, each made expressly for the room and each positioned strategically according to the room's seating. One of the living room's plywood-skin walls reached 25 feet high. Sellers had sunk old wood dowels into it so that it would be possible to climb to the top, where he'd put a high seating platform right in front of one of those breathtaking views. "We'd have 10 people climbing that wall," recalls Sellers. Another living room wall was set at a 45-degree angle and had niches that allowed it to be used like stadium seating. "The house engendered socialization," he adds. "It was a phenomenal party house."

Elsewhere inside, a guest was getting changed in a bedroom. To get back down to the action in the living room level, the bottom floor, she needed to climb the various steps and ladders of the chute that ran vertically through the architecture's bedroom volume. This is how Sellers designed Bridge House—even the spaces designated for sleeping were fun to use and focused on nature. "Every bed was flush with a window," he says, "so when you wake up in the morning you're looking right out at the view. When you went to bed, you were looking at the stars."

PARTINGS

Sellers ultimately held on to Bridge House for several years, alternately using it as his personal ski retreat and as a rental property. In 1978, years after he finally sold the house, having given in to pressure from a frequent renter who was eager to call it his own, Bridge House caught fire and burned to the ground. A wood stove in the lowest level had opened in the middle of the night and coals had spilled onto the plywood floor. There was never any discussion about rebuilding. After all, in form and especially in spirit, this wasn't a house that could ever be duplicated.

> BRIDGE HOUSE. Prickly Mountain, Vermont. Dave Sellers and Edwin Owre, architects, designers, and builders.

DIED: Jan. 18, 1978, The Bridge House, at Prickley Mt., age 12.

Last week the Bridge House burned to the ground. For a handful of afficionados it means the passing of a manifestation of dreams and a massive experiment in exploring space, light, sculpture, color, texture, materials, and man's relation to what he makes.

A wall of bedrooms, a bed cantalevered into the trees, southlight scoops, stressed-skin plywood structures.

Two, 100 foot bridges intersecting in the middle of the house . . .

End grain plywood floors, castings from salvaged farm machinery used as steps, chairs, doorknobs, bowl mill sinks and seats . . .

The 24 foot long single pieces of plastic for a panoramic view . . .

The thirty foot cantalevers and 60 foot spans on the bridges . . . all these were part of the house.

"This house is to the traditional, chalet style lodge as a Raushenberg is to a Turner landscape," (Life Magazine, 1968).

But the most wonderful thing about the house was the manner in which it was built, for it began as a test of the relation of an architect and a sculptor and how they could integrate their skills and talents, the composition of forms, color, texture, and materials, with light, structure, space and function.

First, was to forget about designing the house and go right to building it, so the sculpture is integrated into the action of the form from the beginning.

Starting with sculptor Ed Owre, now on the faculty of the University of Vermont, and architect David Seller, more than a dozen painters, sculptors, and architects from across the United States participated in the creation.

The Bridge House was among the first in a style of action-buildings and reality-oriented artistic statements which are still emerging in the U.S. today.

Speaking for many, we are sorry to see her gone, but the value behind the experience of the house can never be lost, and we are all the better for it.

—David Sellers

ABOVE: Although Sellers says he wasn't interested in Vermont's rich barn vernacular at the time, the clapboard-covered kitchen/dining area had the rough-hewn crudeness that's characteristic of barns—and a defining element of the handmade aesthetic. Parts of old farm equipment (tractor seats mounted on truck springs) became furniture. As in the other rooms, the electrical conduit was left exposed. ABOVE, RIGHT: Years after Sellers sold Bridge House, a fire swept through the building, and it was never rebuilt.

To realize Monte Mano, a getaway on Sardinia for himself and
his wife Veronique, self-trained
architect Jacques Couëlle recruited a team of local artisans
who crafted everything by hand.
Throughout the house, nothing is
uniform or standard; everything
suggests art. THESE PAGES: The
ground-floor living and dining rooms open via pocket doors
leading to gardens and a swimming pool that was poured into
a formation of granite boulders.
The upper-level bedroom converges
with a roof garden. RIGHT: Couëlle
at the Cala di Volpe Hotel, 1960s.

Jacques & Veronique Couëlle

c. 1966–71

INSIDE THE GRANITE SHEPHERD'S hut, a
nineteenth-century Sardinian *stazzi* that's used
as a gatehouse at the Monte Mano property,
is a bulletin board inscribed with dozens of
names and their corresponding local phone
numbers. During the mid-to-late 1960s, while
the house he'd designed for second wife,
Veronique, was being built a hundred yards
away, Jacques Couëlle stayed in this romantic
little structure. Nearly all of the scrawlings on
the browning parchment are from his hand.
Reading them is a journey—a trip back to the
jet-setting origins of the Costa Smeralda, the
one-of-a-kind architecturally focused and ecologically attuned resort development begun in
1961 on 25,000 northeastern Sardinia acres.

    Among the bulletin board's dozens of
entries, one will find "Cala di Volpe," the hotel
Couëlle designed in 1961 that, with its architecture evoking a medieval fishing village and

its artful, crafted embellishments, set the tone on the coast; "Grassetto," the Rome-based construction firm that built the hotel along with most of the area's villas and other early, defining projects; "Cerasarda," the local company launched in 1963 for the sole purpose of crafting tile and other custom ceramics products for those buildings; and "Alisarda," the Sardinian airline started in 1963 in an effort to take the hassle out of getting to the coast. And then the most telling of all contacts: "Aga Khan," or, rather, Prince Karim Aga Khan IV, the leader of the Ismaili Muslims and, as founder of the Costa Smeralda (and the last word on its building designs), the man who made possible each of the phone numbers, not to mention Couëlle's Monte Mano.

LANDINGS

The site was a gift. As part of his compensation, the legend goes, Couëlle, one of the first architects hired for the Costa Smeralda by the Aga Khan, had his pick of locations on which to build for himself. By 1966, he'd made moves in that direction, staking out an isolated hilltop, a typically Sardinian sun-splashed lunar landscape of colossal wind- and wave-shaped granite outcroppings, with clusters of juniper, myrtle, strawberry, and olive trees contributing moments of color and shade. The location's watchful-eye views of Cala di Volpe bay and the hotel made it unique in the area. While working on the hotel, this site, situated more than 800 feet above sea level, would have been in the architect's constant view. He gave in to the beckoning.

Also in '66, the architect unveiled the final scale model of his design for the house. Since the early '60s he'd been advancing his "landscape house" concept. But now, operating as his own client and with the extraordinary materials and old-world talent resources of the Costa Smeralda at his fingertips, he was able to fully stretch artistically. Only a few months earlier, the then-63-year-old architect had told writer Armand Lanoux, "The first house is the mother's womb, with a constant temperature and a liquid ambiance. I would like to build houses in a liquid setting, build them like jellyfish...." While the new house on Sardinia was perched above sea level, its biomorphic shape, akin to any number of marine invertebrates, suggested Couëlle was fast closing in on his goal.

PRECEDENTS

In June of 1964, the *New York Times* published the first in a series of articles that introduced the work of Jacques Couëlle to the world. The stir was Castellaras-le-Neuf, a full-service gated vacation community located on a 110-acre estate in the French Maritime Alps city of Mouans-Sartoux. It was Couëlle's second such project. In '55, the self-trained architect had created Castellaras-le-Vieux, more than 80 Provençal-style houses, each with certain surrealistic tweaks, situated on the same estate. (At the center of this community was his first completed house, a replica of a fifteenth-century French château that Couëlle made almost entirely from period architectural salvage.) Among Castellaras-le-Vieux's early buyers was the Aga Khan's father, Aly Khan. It's probable that the Aga Khan, then a history student at Harvard, would have vacationed there and met Couëlle. It was a fortuitous beginning.

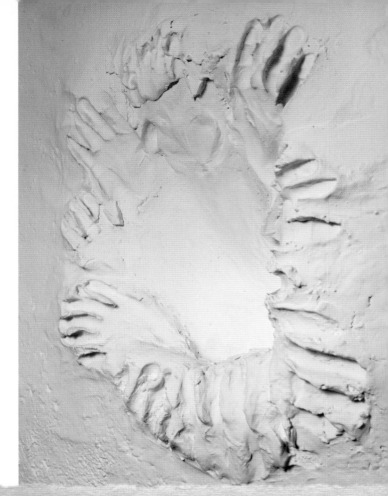

OPPOSITE: The doorway to the living room is the kind of opening that Couëlle would approximate in a scale model and then, during construction and with the structural rebar in hand, sculpt into its final form. His primary design elements (the granite floor, the built-in seating, and the monolithic granite stair to the master bedroom) emphasize natural materials, artistic handcraft, and a comforting sense of permanence. ABOVE: The recessed wall lighting is sculpted into the plaster. The craftsman's handprints, some of which are Couëlle's, become the ornamentation.

But Castellaras-le-Neuf was something else. Its financiers had given the architect creative control.

What Couëlle delivered with the new houses at Castellaras-le-Neuf exploded all expectations and preconceived notions of what was possible. The houses were sculpted "wombs," earthen roofed and punc-

tured with strategically positioned "light canons." The architectural forms were a flashback to Sicily's Pantalica or Cappadocia's Üçhisar Castle. But they were anything but primitive. Each house was assigned its own special team of artists and artisans. These teams crafted custom doors and doorknobs. They designed tiles for the flooring. They made murals and sculptures inside and out. Considering that in the late 1960s these houses were going for between $160,000 and $200,000, "radical" didn't even begin to cover what Couëlle was doing.

"The floor of a building can be level, but all the rest must be movement," the architect said. "My houses are living beings … they have a nervous system, a stomach, intestines, a heart. They are built like madreporic sponges." The houses were thrilling. But the concept, selling idiosyncratic, high-art handcrafted houses to the rich, was groundbreaking.

In October 1965, the *New York Times* dispatched its new architecture critic, Ada Louise Huxtable, to Castellaras for an in-depth assessment of Couëlle's work. "A house that is at once a home, and a sophisticated work of art," wrote Huxtable in her review, calling each dwelling "a giant piece of sculpture." Huxtable continued: "[Each] is molded in rosy reinforced concrete into striking free forms that emerge from the site and hug its contours to bring the sense of landscape indoors, dramatically echoing its colors and curves. Fountains cascade down handcrafted façades; roof gardens spill over shaggy walls; dreamlike forms tread a delicate line between Disneyland and sophisticated esthetic design." While much of the architectural establishment in the United States was still hanging on to Modernism's machine aesthetic, Couëlle was reviving the craft tradition and integrating structure and nature in ways that Modern architecture's icons had never achieved.

like a sculptor. He'd get inside the framework and make sure he had accurately predicted the views and the light penetration. At any given moment, he might order the complete disassembly and reworking of a major feature. Since Castellaras, this had been his process. "For just when the masons thought they had a shell finished to Couëlle's satisfaction," the *New York Times* reported, "the architect would dash on the scene, cast an eye on the setting sun, then reach up and chalk the outlines of some wildly irregular shape (which Couëlle insisted was a window) on a wall and order, 'Cut here.'"

ARCHAEOLOGY BEFORE ARCHITECTURE

In the 1940s, Couëlle ran a Paris-based company called the Research Center for Natural Structure. "I was seeking the secret architecture of organized bodies," was how he described its agenda. "We were subsidized by industries, for example, to discover a tire which could not blow out," he told historian Michel Ragon. "We devoted our investigations at that time to elephants' feet. By studying the shells of tortoises, we were able to improve the hulls of boats. Whales' bellies gave us some leads for partitions." Nearly thirty years later he was obviously still referencing the results of those progressive studies, if not building on them. His Research Center's work is the key to understanding the awakening he had while

THE DIRECTOR

During the construction of Monte Mano, as was Couëlle's practice, the scale model was the reference point used on-site, in place of any drawings. With the building's sinuous footprint marked off, the construction crew would bend and twist the rebar into the shapes Couëlle had articulated in the model. Then, in preparation for the sprayed concrete, meshlike metal lath would be laid over the rebar. During the shaping of the structural steel, Couëlle would often be on the site with a megaphone in hand, directing the shaping of the forms designing the Castellaras communities, when he went from reinventing the past, as he'd done with the Provençal-style houses there, to reinventing the present. His own house on Sardinia was the next advancement.

LA VITA DELLA SARDEGNA

By 1971, Monte Mano was mostly complete. For Couëlle, the period of its construction had included regular commutes between Sardinia, his residences in Redon, France, and Paris, and work in locations such as Monaco, Martinique, and Senegal. Meanwhile, local carpenter Niccola Azzara, Couëlle's foreman on the Hotel Cala di Volpe, saw to it that Monte Mano's detailing was done according to the architect's exacting specifications and that the gardens were flourishing. A team of artisans applied the handmade Robert Picault–designed Cerasarda handmade tiles that clad the façade like fish scales. They finessed the phosphor bronze sheeting that covers portions of the façade like whale's skin. They hammered the copper that covers the interior doors. They set the massive rough-cut granite stair treads in the living room and honed the room's granite floor tiles. The layers go on and on, all of them done by hand.

Throughout the rest of the '70s, Jacques and Veronique resided here intermittently, during which time they opened Monte Mano's doors to a who's who list of artists and actors and models and other celebrities. (The architect counted Salvador Dalí and Pablo Picasso among his circle of friends.) In 1982, the couple put the house on the market and returned to Paris. In 1996, at age 93, Couëlle died.

Two subsequent owners have experienced living at Monte Mano, and each has left his mark on it and

been deeply affected by it. The old bulletin board in the gatehouse remains the same, however, treated like a time capsule in the service of the Couëlle legend and the early days of this beautiful place.

From the beach at the Hotel Cala di Volpe, it's still possible to catch glimpses of Couëlle's handmade house on the hill, which is only fitting; for, as the architect once told Ragon, "The house is not made alone for he who *lives* in it but also for he who *looks* at it."

MONTE MANO. Jacques Couëlle, architect. Niccola Azzara, principal builder and craftsperson. Robert Picault, ceramics.

British Columbia's Henry Yorke Mann, an architect and engineer with heavy-timber carpentry skills in his blood, disregarded much of what the architecture profession dictated and, instead, led the way in soulful health- and eco-conscious solid-wood architecture. Not one to improvise on-site, Mann's "every piece is important because every piece is exposed" philosophy depends on profusely detailed working drawings. Typical of his buildings, the 1,650-square-foot Clark House in West Vancouver packs a lot of design into its responsibly small footprint. THESE PAGES: The front elevation. RIGHT: Hilary Clark and her children, 1969.

Hilary & David Clark

with Henry Yorke Mann

THE NOVEMBER DAY IN 1966 when Hilary and David Clark knocked at the door of architect Henry Mann and then-wife poet Judy Copithorne's North Vancouver house for the first time, they found their fate waiting for them inside. Hilary had only recently discovered Mann's work in an article on his residence featured in the October 1965 issue of *Western Homes and Living*. The architect, along with his brother, Richard H. Mann, and their master-builder father, Richard P. Mann, had constructed this 700-square-foot, woodsy-Modern box for a mere $7,000. An exercise in low-cost, health-conscious design and construction, the 1958 Mann House, Henry's first major solo project following his architecture

OPPOSITE: For health reasons, the house is built entirely of fir. Mann's master-builder father, Richard P. Mann, is responsible for most of the craftsmanship, although several Vietnam War conscientious objectors from California also contributed. The wood is treated with linseed oil but otherwise left natural. ABOVE: Hilary Clark in the dining room, 2010.

Floors were covered with wool felt that the architect recycled from local paper mills. There wasn't an inch of Sheetrock.

Like the architect's later works, the Mann House was a breathable building, purposely conceived to avoid the so-called sick-home syndrome. "Everything about it seemed to be a good idea," says Hilary, who was then exploring options for the making of a new house. "It was simple. It was solid wood. It was all right down on the floor, sort of Japanese style. I just loved that. I was moving into this freedom from my extremely rigid, British upbringing—everything was square and everything was proper. And this whole hippie thing opened up a completely new approach. And I think that's why I was so open to Henry's designing. I recall thinking, 'Oh my God! This is all possible? This beautiful piece of sculpture—I can live in this?' It was amazing. And he was a very, very exciting person." The house that an architect designs and builds for himself often is a repository of all his ideas, and Mann's house was exactly that. Hilary was entirely won over by what she saw, and given the health challenges of her children, she could accept nothing less.

THE "GOD DANCE"

Some houses are conceived for vanity's sake. Others are borne out of a simple need for shelter. The design and construction of the Clark House, however, was a matter of life or death. "My two sons had severe, severe allergies. I almost lost the second one," explains Hilary. "And so the more we looked at existing houses, dust was a consideration, mold was a consideration, the kind of heating was a consideration. Everything was something for these

and engineering training at Washington State and the University of Oregon, suggested a "green" approach before there was such a term. It was also a pioneering example of what's now known as design-build. The structure's walls, floors, and roof were built using only locally sourced 3-inch-thick Douglas fir or cedar—all of it paint free, outside and inside.

seriously ill children. They had dust allergies as well as contact allergies as well as food allergies as well as drug allergies. We started thinking that maybe we should build, and then we'd get a house that is allergy free, because that would be one of the criteria." A verdant, creekside ⅓-acre lot in West Vancouver was found and acquired and, in January of 1967, with a budget of $28,000, Mann went to work. The first drawings he produced, presented just before the Stanley Park Be-In, were accompanied by a poem he'd written about the design. The final verse promised a house that would be concerned with "intensifying the God Dance Experience."

Mann used to tell his draftsmen, "You have to do the working drawings with a holy state of mind. Because that's where all the finishing touches come in." When the Clark House's drawings were finally completed, certain touches had gone through considerable transformation. By necessity, late in the design phase the floor plan went from incorporating three bedrooms to having a tightly squeezed four. The Clark family was growing again.

STEADFASTNESS

By late 1968, John Senac, Mann's partner in Senac
& Mann Construction, had visited the local timber-
processing grounds and had hand-selected the fir logs
that would be cut for the house's construction. David
and Hilary's West Vancouver lot was now buzzing
with activity, but this wasn't an ordinary construction
scene. Standing on the property, between the stacks
of timber, equipment, and supplies, were tents—the
temporary homes of some of the workers. "We were
part of the silent railway coming up from California with all the Vietnam War draft dodgers," Hilary
explains. "We were Unitarians at that point. I'm not
but my husband was. The church would take them in
and we'd find them somewhere to stay. Over time, we
employed about 30 of them as journeymen when we
were building this house, and they lived here throughout that process."

Another unique presence was David Clark, who
tirelessly visited the site daily, after his own normal
working hours, to clean and apply a preservative to the
wood that was being prepared for the next day and to
vacuum out all the debris, "because we didn't want to
build in construction dust along with everything else,
because of the dust allergies," Hilary says. "He was
cutting costs but it practically killed him." Meanwhile,
as the structure grew, the neighbors, with their comparatively staid houses, looked on with dumbfounded
amazement. "They thought we were nuts," says Hilary.
"They used to come by and call it the hydrogen bomb
shelter!" Real pressure and stress gripped the Clarks,
however, when in the middle of the building process
they learned they'd gone double over budget. In the
midst of her pregnancy, Hilary got a job teaching at the
local college, started selling her sand-cast candles,
and began writing about crafts for *Canadian Homes*
magazine. She wasn't short on determination.

GIANT LEAPS

Five months after NASA's Neil Armstrong stepped onto the surface of the moon, on Christmas Day 1969, David and Hilary and their three boys moved into their new home. They came armed with little more than their bags and, appropriately enough, a fully decorated Christmas tree. Still raw and somewhat incomplete, the house hadn't even been seen by the final building inspector. Where the glass doors were supposed to be, plywood was temporarily hung. But that didn't matter; by this point the family had seen tough times, and they jumped at the first chance to get out of financial commitments to their temporary living arrangements and into the house that they'd overextended themselves to complete. It was a bittersweet beginning.

"The angst around building this thing was so horrendous that I really hated the house," says Hilary. "But as I got to live with it and put some color into it and got some paintings up, I began to love it. But that first year, we'd sacrificed too much to get Henry his dream. Though his dream was brilliant."

CALLINGS

By the time of Mann's start on the Clark House, he'd evolved his own manner of heavy-timber architecture through the completion of several single-family houses. Mann could do architecture, engineering, and carpentry with equal skill. Brushstrokes of Frank Lloyd Wright and Bernard Maybeck were evident in his work, as were certain aspects of Tibetan, Japanese, and Vietnamese vernacular structures. The heavy post-and-beam and solid-wood building he conceived for the Clarks represented a new creative frontier for the architect. But when he finished it, he sold his own place and walked away from architecture and construction altogether. For the next three years, he homesteaded a 40-acre plot in the Squamish River Valley, living in a tent with no electricity. "I felt I had advanced in my headspace a little bit more than I could handle, and I needed some time away from it," Mann says. In 1972, he started cattle ranching in the Okanagan Hills. Mann's back-to-the-land lifestyle continued until 1997, when he finally returned to architecture.

CENTERING

Today, when Hilary Clark traverses the bridge that spans the creek in front of her driveway, she greets the house that she, personally, has lovingly preserved since 1969. Divorced for several of those years, she ended up buying out her ex-husband in order to keep the house, and she couldn't be happier about it. From time to time she shares that joy, opening the home to local tours of significant architecture. With her background in interior design, she tends to give visitors an expert run-through. "I go through the bit that it's a cruciform shape and the stairs meet in the center, and so it's a centered house," she says. "And I explain that all the rooms are terminal, except the dining room, so you don't go through rooms to get to other rooms." The skylight-equipped 12' x 12' conversation area, what Mann says is "basically a mandala," appears to float above the other rooms of the second floor and, for visitors, is inevitably one of the open-plan interior's more fascinating features. "I'm living in an art object, and I love art," summarizes Hilary. "You can't look anywhere here without having an aesthetic experience, and that really turns me on."

CLARK HOUSE. West Vancouver, Canada, BC. Henry Yorke Mann, architect. Senac & Mann Construction, builder.

"So much of what's touted as a 'green' building is currently as dull as dishwater with little sense of architectural structure," Mann says. "These buildings—Modern and green—with their lack of warmth and humanity, leave our souls unsatisfied." Mann calls this house "spiritual green." THIS PAGE: The driveway entrance, where the kitchen peeks out from the trees.

A private cove in Malibu filled
with multimillion-dollar homes
is an unlikely location for
a handmade house, much less
a classic example of one—but
Harry Gesner's place more than
holds its own. THESE PAGES:
The tower with its reclaimed
stained-glass windows contains
the second-floor master suite
and the third-level drafting
studio. The ground floor's
original cedar-shake roof
proved too great a fire hazard.
OPPOSITE: Gesner and his late
wife, actress Nan Martin, 1974.

Harry & Nan Gesner

c. 1970

THE SILVER 1960 MERCEDES 300SL convertible was roaring up the Pacific Coast Highway, bound with determination for a secluded cove at the far end of Malibu. Like the full moon that lit the way, the driver, Harry Gesner, Los Angeles architect and man-about-town, was beaming. Earlier that day he'd reconnected with his dream girl. The award-winning actress of stage and screen Nan Martin had captivated Gesner since their days as classmates at Santa Monica High School. They'd gone their separate ways into adulthood, but now, on June 15, 1968, more than 20 years later, she was seated beside him in his prized two-seater. The top was down. The stars were out. Everything was looking up.

A lifelong surfer, Gesner focused on ecology long before the 1969 Santa Barbara oil spill—an event that contributed to the escalating environmental movement. But back then, he says, his preference for used windows and hardware from Victorian-era buildings and patinated old timber had more to do with aesthetics: "They made houses much more warm and personable." THESE PAGES: The living room fireplace, a riff on the Hollywood Bowl, was built from used bricks. OPPOSITE TOP: A window rescued from a Pasadena church lights the greenhouse. OPPOSITE BOTTOM: In the master suite, a spiral stair made from local driftwood connects to the studio.

"We got there and parked right above the vacant lot," Gesner recalls. "You could see clear down to the beach where the house now sits, and I said, 'Nan, if you marry me,'—I just blurted it right out—'I will design and build you a home on that site down there.'" Martin could see the lot but she didn't see this coming. "She was dumbfounded!" says Gesner. "She was supposed to leave the next day and return to New York. She was starring in a motion picture called *For Love of Ivy*, with Sydney Poitier, Beau Bridges, and Carroll O'Connor. She had a full plate. And I was

really interrupting! So she doesn't answer my question. She says, 'I'll think about it.' Later on that night, she said, 'I'm shipping my things from New York!'"

CLOSE ACQUAINTANCE

The empty stretch of Malibu beachfront that became the home of Harry Gesner and Nan Martin—newly-weds—and, eventually, their son together, Zen Gesner, would've scared off many potential buyers. Wedged between the PCH and the lot is a near-sheer cliff, a

70-foot vertical drop, with a single, precarious one-lane road leading down to the beach via a hairpin turn. It wouldn't be possible to get conventional lift equipment down there for construction purposes. An underground spring cut through the property, compromising the integrity of the towering cliff behind the lot. But this wasn't Gesner's first time at the cove. Since the 1950s, it'd been his surf spot.

In '61, upon receiving the commission to design the neighboring house to the east, the Cooper House, the architect came up with his own ways of studying the site's natural features to determine what would best complement them: One day he arrived with his surfboard and a wax pencil tucked into his trunks. He paddled straight out beyond the little breakers in front of the lot and, while sitting there afloat, he sketched onto the deck of his 12-foot Velzy-Jacobs the elevations of the house that he would help build and that would go on to be celebrated in *Life* magazine for its daring design. When the opportunity arrived to create a house of his own on this beach, a project he started designing in '68, "moments after Nan said, 'yes,'" Gesner didn't need to get wet.

PURITY

Gesner was 42 when he and his small crew poured the foundation and began laying the concrete-block retaining wall of the three-bedroom, three-bath Sand-castle and the matching detached house for son Zen. To get up and running with the project, he'd sold the rare Mercedes. Money was tight, but not creativity. In order to get the house done, Gesner took two years off from working for anyone else and swore he wouldn't shave or cut his hair until it was finished. What Gesner, long hair and all, came up with combines aspects of Gothic, Victorian, and Modern styles, as well as the California ranch- and Japanese folk-house vernaculars. Traits of the central European medieval castles that he saw during World War II and maritime themes are a part of it too. The resulting fusion, however, is the Gesnerian design vocabulary—every bit of it under one roof.

"I couldn't miss," Gesner explains, surveying what he'd conceived while sitting on this beach 40 years ago, "because I did all the creative conceptual work on-site, as I always do. I kept going to circles, to circles within circles. I wasn't thinking of a lighthouse necessarily, although that may have had a part in it. I wasn't thinking of a windmill either, and it ended up looking a lot like a Greek windmill."

ESSENCE

Gesner's Sandcastle is the kind of house that's entered through the back door. To get there, you must first walk down a steep, cypress-blanketed cliffside. The choreography gives glimpses of the orange, yellow, and blue antique stained-glass windows that mark a side of the house's white stucco tower; then the horizon; and then the Pacific, with a purple kelp bed and a sailboat or two drifting in and out of the picture. Finally, once you've made it all the way down the steep driveway lined with driftwood logs and boulders, a complete view of the house's profile unfolds: The ground floor is a canonical dome supported by a rafter system of curved heavy beams, the tails of which are carved and extend well past the deep sheltering eaves, continuing the Japan-esque roofline's upturn. Its exterior walls alternate between rough-sawn cedar boards and triangular bats and wide panels of floor-to-ceiling glass framed in reclaimed mahogany. An attached greenhouse on the southwest side has Tiffany stained glass that Gesner and onetime Malibu Fire Department chief Dutch Clansey hauled out of a Pasadena church that was being demolished. Rising out of the center of the dome is the three-story white stucco tower that defines the profile.

But it's through the back door that you enter the heart of this house, the circular domed kitchen. Like the recycled and uncreosoted telephone poles that serve as posts throughout, and the living and dining area's 100-year-old bird's-eye maple floorboards that Gesner salvaged from a burned-down turn-of-the-century school gymnasium, *and* the living-area doors that came out of an old movie theater on Hollywood Boulevard, *and* the door hardware that came from dilapidated Victorians in downtown L.A., the Gesner kitchen has a story behind it.

"The gas company financed it and the *Los Angeles Times* did a spread on it," he explains. "Before we built this house, they called me down to the *Times* and asked me if I would design 'the ultimate kitchen.' I didn't know how much work was going to go into it but nevertheless I did it. So they built it, and it cost them at least $100,000." In the end, as payment, he received his entire project back—the John Wallis leaded-glass ceiling, the round island that

allows knives and other tools to be simply dropped lengthwise into storage slots bored into its butcher-block top, all the latest appliances, all the custom ash cabinetry, the chocolate ceramic-tile countertops. Gesner conceived the open-beam kitchen around these features. A curved fireplace with a medieval hammered-copper hood, which he positioned at countertop level, was the finishing architectural touch.

To a great extent, the essence of the house is contained in the kitchen's architecture, the symbol of the circle. But it's also revealed in the textures and patinas of the unpainted recycled woods that he used; the colorful braided rugs that Nan's mother made; the worn 1946 Eames plywood dining chairs at the breakfast bar; the walls dedicated to family photos; a hat collection and their many awards and commendations; and the framed cover of the April 1948 issue of *Vogue* magazine that features Nan. She died on March 9, 2010.

MIRRORS

Thinking back over his childhood here, Zen Gesner remembers that his father would always light a fire in the living room, the main fireplace, and that fire would warm the whole house. Gesner explains, "He'd always say that it did that because the house was round, and the fire radiated heat from the bowl-core of it outward, to every room and floor within. I understood his reasoning, but then I realized there was another level to my father's design: One stormy night, as I looked out from the hearth in front of a roaring fire, I noticed that the fire was reflected in every window of the room. He had designed the living room to reflect the fire's light and magnify its beauty and warmth a hundred times over. With a storm raging outside, I never felt safer and warmer than at that moment. My father had seen that visual effect in the design, and he knew the calming and magical effect it would have on your soul. To me, that is the essence of his work, the embodiment of his nature." This kind of orchestrating, evident throughout the house, is not unique to Gesner. He just does it with more verve than most architects.

UP WITH THE SUN, OUT WITH THE TIDE

The surf in front of the Sandcastle has been good lately, and despite being 84 and having a number of design projects running full tilt, Harry still hasn't missed a day in the water. Reaching down to pick up a moonstone lodged between two hunks of jade half-buried in the sand just beyond the tide line, his surfboard tucked under his arm after yet another morning session, Gesner shares a parting thought about the house: "From the very beginning, as the concept took shape in my mind's eye, I knew it was going to be unique—a fabulous place to live and make love within, a place that would be a part of us for the rest of our lives."

THE SANDCASTLE. Malibu, California. Harry H. Gesner, architect, builder, interior designer.

With a strong cinematic romanticism, the Sandcastle finds its fullest expression when the setting sun begins to reflect off the Pacific. BELOW: Over the original garage, at left, Gesner built an apartment for his son, Zen.

Val Agnoli has the uncommon ability to construct the
radical houses he designs. In his 40-plus-year career as
an architect, taking on the carpentry and construction too
was frequently his only option to ensure his drawings were
properly followed. For the Rock House in Stinson Beach,
built with Vietnam War dunnage on "a throw-away kind
of lot" that he acquired for $7,500, he wanted it all to
himself. THESE PAGES: The view from the driveway. OPPOSITE:
The architect-builder in his studio.

Valentino Agnoli

c. 1971

THE REVERBERATING SONG of Val Agnoli's handsaw rang out through the thick early-morning Stinson Beach fog. In this sleepy community of fewer than 500 full-time residents, it didn't cross the architect-builder's mind that his work might disturb anyone within earshot, including Jerry Garcia of the Grateful Dead and his wife, Mountain Girl, the residents of the house just up the hill. Stinson Beach was, after all, a place you came to in order to be left to your own devices with your creativity. And at this moment in the fall of 1971, out on this rock-covered mountainside overlooking the Pacific Ocean and three miles of sandy beach, Agnoli, the staunchly individualistic artist's architect and former student of Bruce Goff, was indeed alone. On a lot that cost him $7,500, he was constructing one of his own designs entirely his way, with no assistance. He

was doing it without electricity, relying on hand tools instead. If that made things more challenging, at least the building codes were lenient. Which meant he wouldn't be forced to stick to a script. Improvisation—in design and in construction—could and, in the Goff tradition, would play an important part. Having recently dropped out of the San Francisco scene, fleeing the grind and the banalities that characterized the typical corporate architectural practice at that time, Agnoli, at age 42, had managed to situate himself on the edge—right where he wanted to be.

ELEMENTAL EMPHASIS

"The rock formations determined just about everything," Agnoli says, looking back at the house today with 40 years of hindsight. "I just wanted to nestle up against the rocks and sort of put a roof over them and, sometimes, a plastic greenhouse treatment. I didn't overwhelm the site with construction. I didn't try to obliterate the identity of the site by pouring tons of concrete. It was all mixed by hand—very small, well-thought-out, well-reinforced concrete elements. Not having electricity and doing everything physically helped establish the lightness. In fact, the building

Inside: slender reclaimed timbers, natural rock formations, and Plexiglas. Agnoli sought only the most minimal sense of enclosure, and so instead of walls hung with art there are nature views—explosive, near and far. THESE PAGES: The kitchen/ dining area with its original Douglas fir cabinetry around the sink and stove. LEFT: He used most of the dunnage without sanding it, leaving the military stamps in place for later storytelling.

became so light in proportion to the density of the rock that it was almost nonexistent. We would have sat there and lived on that site, with the rocks, if you didn't need protection from the sun and the rain and the cold." It was a case of trying to achieve a lot with as little as possible—an approach that, by today's standards, would be entirely counterintuitive.

WAR TORN TO REBORN

Plexiglas transparency characterizes much of the economical structure, but Agnoli also used an abundance of timber. And instead of relying on the newly milled materials available from the local lumberyard, he and a friend got in his one-ton Chevrolet Suburban and drove to Oakland, California, where ships returning from the Vietnam War were depositing their dunnage. "I kind of liked the idea of recycling these things that were coming back from the war," says Agnoli. "All this wood was dumped in one gigantic pile, and for five dollars you could fill up a pickup truck's worth. So we stacked it up. There were a lot of beautiful exotic woods there—mahoganies and also fir from this country. Some of it was stenciled with the word *Da Nang*. There's still one beam in the house that has that on it."

NATURAL PROCESSION

At the front of the property, a simple, ornament-free wood stair constructed with the precision of Japanese joinery moves through a shady grove of bansai bay laurel trees and descends the slope, concluding at the front door of the house. Once inside, Agnoli's cliffside-greenhouse concept immediately unfolds, level by level, as the structure drops gently down the mountain toward the view. The variations in level height encourage frequent movement, making the compact floor plan feel dynamic and more expansive than its actual footprint would suggest. As you move from room to room, floor-to-ceiling windows set up infinitely varied vistas of the coastline and Mount Tamalpais.

Save for the fire-surround area, which is painted, all the wood components—mullions, posts, beams, ceiling structure, cabinets—are exposed and left health-consciously naked, their natural patinas radiating warmth. But it is the bare rocks and the precision

OPPOSITE: The fact that he was working alone and on a steep site determined the materials and construction solutions. When he needed a large timber, as he did when assembling the post-and-beam structure seen in the living room, he'd make a substitute by laminating smaller ones. BELOW: The master bedroom.

About a decade after they moved into the Rock
House, with their children nearing adolescence, the
Kirsches enclosed the original open-air shower with
cedar. The new construction, which takes its cues
from Agnoli, keeps the back-to-the-land feel.

with which Agnoli's design and construction strategically incorporates them that make this house so
unforgettable. "The experience of living there," he
points out, "is that you are exposed to rock. And that
must do something to people. It's kind of an anchoring device in a way—this is something you're not
going to change." A dominant feature of almost every
room, the rocks are also a calming presence. They're
essential to the success of the architecture, serving it
both functionally and ornamentally.

PROSPECT

Agnoli and wife Tamae lived here only for a matter of months, eventually opting to use it as a rental
property. In 1976, after it had hosted a succession of
tenants, the Rock House ended up with its present
owners, Charles and Margaux Kirsch. Following an
extended stay in Japan, the newly married couple
had just returned home to Stinson Beach and were
seeking a place to call their own together. A few
serendipitous events had led Charles to those stairs
at the front, where he was promptly seduced by the
Rock House's "million-dollar view." The rent? $400.
"I came up to see where we were now going to live,"
recalls Margaux, "and I remember thinking, 'Oh, I just
want to keep my old house down the hill and preserve
this house exactly as it is,' because it was so pure and
so calm and so serene—and without any attachments.
There was nothing to it but trees, vast views, and the
simplicity. The cottage just kept taking advantage
of every part of nature, wherever you stood." This is
not the typical Stinson weekender. No other house in
town was as daring. Likewise, no other house had the
same quality-of-life potential. But you had to be able
to see past the total disregard for "normal."

HERE WE ARE IN THE YEARS

By the mid-1980s, Charles, a small-business owner,
and Margaux, a fashion designer who was part of the
national art-clothing movement, had acquired the
house from Agnoli and were raising their children
there. The kitchen was small but served as the family
hearth, constantly in service. "Children, friends,

and family filled the kitchen for meals and gatherings always hungry, and everyone was fed," Margaux notes. "I've always said that I could go right from this kitchen to a sailboat kitchen and make Thanksgiving dinner for 10." To this day, that room of the house remains largely as Agnoli designed and built it, complete with its custom-crafted cabinets made out of recycled wood and that beam stamped with the word *Da Nang*. Only the floor has been altered, the present bamboo having replaced the original edge-out 2' x 4' flooring. In an age when many residential kitchens are exercises in grandiosity, Margaux chooses to keep the small-scale integrity of hers intact.

The interiors recall Japan. For Margaux, who did the decorating and who has long held a strong affinity for Japanese art and fashion, that kind of quiet minimalism belongs here. "When we arrived, this house had bits of Japanese aesthetic already, like the shoji screen that separates the bedroom from the living room," she explains. "I followed my passion for ancient Japanese temples and homes, continuing what was already here. It really is about looking out, not necessarily looking at furniture or objects. Our walls are windows filled with trees, mountains, ocean, and sky." Agnoli's concept is fulfilling its promise, but only because the house ended up with the right owners.

"I always wanted to do the right thing by this house," Margaux adds, "to pay my respects to the natural beauty by keeping it uncluttered and by directing one's eye to the views. Val was told the land was unbuildable. I'm so glad he didn't listen." The house's essence is almost palpable for her. It's something she takes great pride in sharing. "Everyone feels their own personal peacefulness here," she says. It's an attribute that's built in—made possible by the simple fact that this house was designed and built by one individual and with the right energy and intention.

ESSENTIALS

On a brisk but bright Stinson Beach winter afternoon in 2010, Agnoli is seated by the fireplace in his living room, in another house of his design and construction, examining a series of recent photographs of the Rock House. "It taught me a lot," he says. "And I had a lot of beautiful times just being there. It makes me feel good, because as a country, as a culture, we use a heavy hand with everything. We overeat, overbuild, overwaste, and overconsume. And that house, it gets back to a kind of New England frugality—how much do you really need to put on your plate, nutritionally and also spiritually?"

Charles and Margaux Kirsch and their dog in the living room immediately after they moved in, 1976.

ROCK HOUSE. Stinson Beach, California. Valentino Agnoli, architect and builder. Margaux Kirsch, interior designer.

Michael McNamara & Family

c. 1972-73

THE PLAN WAS TO SPEND THE NIGHT in the Corvair and then, the next morning, start a new life. Michael McNamara and his girlfriend, Kirsten Humpherys, had pulled their "camperized" van into Vancouver's Stanley Park and turned the engine off at a little point overlooking the Salish Sea. They had their minds on catching the sunset and, moreover, bringing to an end what had been an extraordinarily long and eventful day. Just as they were settling in, a police car pulled up beside them. " 'Oh fuck, here we go,' I remember thinking, expecting something extremely unpleasant or possibly dangerous," says McNamara. "But, no, the officer just wanted to tell us that this wasn't the best place to spend the night, because we 'would be sure to be disturbed.' He suggested that if we were to go up a nearby side road we'd find a much more private spot. He also let us know we would be checked on by one of his colleagues during the night. Amazing!"

McNamara's jitters and astonishment were more than justified. Earlier that same August day, 1969, he'd packed his belongings at his home in Portland, Oregon, and closed the door—to the house and to that phase of his life—for what, he'd been certain, would be the last time. He'd recently come home from his job at a local architecture practice to discover in his mailbox a United States Selective Service System draft notice—the third he'd received in as many years. Because he was in the workforce and no longer a student at the University of Oregon, there would be no third deferment. The 26-year-old was expected to report for induction in September, but that, he decided, wasn't going to happen.

"We had really good draft counseling at the U of O," McNamara says. "I mean, you knew exactly what your situation was—what your rights were and what the choices were. So basically my choices were to go into the military and definitely go to Vietnam, given what was going on in 1969. Or I could go to jail. Or I could leave the country. So I decided that I would leave the country. I didn't really have time to be sentimental about the move. Plus I was completely fed up with the political and social situation in the United States at the time—highly polemic, right against left, rednecks against hippies, Black Panthers flexing their power, and seemingly everyone armed to the teeth. War, war, and more war. No civility, no trust. It was way more violent than I wanted to get into." And so there he was that Summer of Love morning, at the United States' border with Vancouver, Canada, waiting in line to get on with his life. An hour later, finally and with relative ease, it was complete: McNamara, just as some 70,000 other Americans had done by 1972 upon receiving their draft orders, became not a U.S. combat soldier in Vietnam but a Canadian landed immigrant. Freedom enveloped him.

In 1970, Michael McNamara was one of several young architect-carpenters who were lured to Hornby Island, British Columbia, by its DIY driftwood architecture and back-to-the-land living. His late 1960s work for Modernist Arthur Erickson and his interest in humble old West Coast barns—and the high-art riffs on them by architects such as Charles Moore and Donlyn Lyndon—helped shape a Hornby handmade aesthetic that was just beginning to gel. THIS PAGE: The front elevation of his house. Beachcombed poles dance with woodbutcher shakes and a window made by McNamara. OPPOSITE: McNamara and wife Sally Campbell, 2011.

SEEDBEDS

Stretched out between Vancouver and Vancouver
Island are the otherworldly Gulf Islands and their
innumerable islets. Most of these landmasses are
sparsely populated and distanced such that access is
possible by boat only. Throughout the chain, nature's
integrity is largely unadulterated. This is especially so
on Hornby Island. When McNamara, Humpherys, and
their friends Dean Ellis and Marylou Moyer first ventured together from their shared house in Vancouver
to Hornby for a consciousness-expanding camping
trip in May of 1970, they found a back-to-the-lander's
paradise. Ellis, an artist, led the way. For months he'd

been raving to McNamara about Hornby's wild, emer-
ald beauty and its improvisational driftwood architecture—a few houses by Canadian master builder Lloyd
House. At that time, the 11.55-square-mile island had
only about 250 full-time residents—loggers, farmers,
fishermen, and a few reclusive intellectuals.

Strolling through Hornby's silent old-growth
Douglas-fir forests, the friends quickly discovered
a bounty of edible wild greens. They combed its
driftwood-strewn beaches and, during low tide, found
an "endless" supply of oysters. After the foraging, they
fashioned an open-fire barbeque and had a communal
feast under starry skies. They also made it to Helliwell
Park, where "a spectacular wildflower explosion" on

the bluffs had McNamara down on his hands and knees with a magnifying glass. "I was into sacred geometry back then and was finding all sorts of deep and meaningful cosmic stuff as I rooted around there," he recalls with amusement. And they visited Leaf House (1969), the masterly designed and ingeniously constructed little cabin by Lloyd House that would inspire so many of the island's woodbutcher-style buildings. It was all McNamara needed to see. He knew he wanted out of the city, and now he'd found the place. It was time to buy land and put down roots.

LITTORAL CONNECTIONS

In August 1972, six massive fir poles were painstakingly being moved into place in a picturesque level clearing on Hornby. McNamara and Ellis's persistence had finally paid off. Together, they had acquired 10 acres on the island. By this point, Ellis had already erected his place, a prefabricated dome, on his 5-acre plot. On the other half of the property, McNamara, at 29 years old and with a budget of "$0 to not very much," was now building a house for himself and Humpherys. The design he was working with existed only in his head; no

architectural drawings were ever produced for the construction. He knew where he was going, though. While at the University of Oregon, McNamara had watched with excitement as the graduate students improvised the construction of a student center using laminated 2 x 4s and peeled poles. In his travels thereafter, he began to really admire the simplicity of the pole structure and the "elegance" of West Coast pole barns and barn forms in general. "At the time," he says, "I was disillusioned with preconceived drawing-board

solutions. And I was reading everything I could get my hands on about traditional Japanese domestic architecture as well as barns. I mean, this is the kind of stuff we were all really fascinated with back then. So that's kind of what I was responding to with this place."

The structural poles were driftwood that McNamara and a few friends had gathered from a Hornby beach. Several thousand board feet of 2 x 4s, obtained for a mere $39 per thousand from a Vancouver Island mill, came next. Other materials were harder won. "We were constantly scrounging for good deals on whatever we needed, and we were trading and bartering," McNamara says. "We'd go to the cities, to Victoria and Vancouver, and raid the building-salvage places and get used windows and the usual things." As for the actual building work, most of it he was doing alone. Once the pole structure was up and reinforced, he built the laminated 2' x 4' roof and floor. "If you're working by yourself," he points out, "you do a lot of scaffolding and rigging, so that you can hoist things up. I had a really nice chain hoist. I'd made an A-frame. So I could raise a couple of tons with perfect control." One-man heavy-timber construction isn't for the faint of heart. Catastrophes lurk behind every move. Yet the young architect-builder kept pushing on.

UNIFIED WHOLES

Over a period of about nine months, "in fits and starts," the first incarnation of the two-story house got built, and it happened without electricity to power the equipment. "It was all hand tools and a chain saw," the architect says. "We had a lot of fun going around and finding old, high-quality hand tools. And everybody around here did a lot of chain-saw carpentry."

The floor plan consisted of a living/dining area on one side and, opposite the salvaged transformer that was made into a wood-burning stove, a kitchen and pantry. A ship's ladder provided access to a skylight-equipped open sleeping loft on the upper level. Because McNamara gave the living/dining area a wide wall of pocket windows and wrapped much of the exterior's perimeter with wood decking, the interiors could grow substantially in spring and summer, effectively becoming a continuous space with the adjacent gardens and the forest beyond. The cedar-shake-clad barn aesthetic turned out to be a perfect marriage with the site.

LONGEVITY

During the couple's first night in the house, their first child, Jessica, was conceived—"as far as we can figure out," McNamara says. She was also born in the house's living room. For their first two years there, the young family lived without electricity, telephone, or an indoor bathroom. But then, with a second daughter, Miriam, on the way, it was time to expand. Staying true to the look of the original design, McNamara added on a bathroom, two bedrooms, and a workshop. It also became the location of his thriving architecture practice, Blue Sky Design, the firm he launched in 1973. "It's interesting to build a place when you're pretty young and then to live there for so many years," he reflects. "I think I've lived here for 40 years." The house is historically significant now but it's no relic. It's about happy continuation.

These days, McNamara shares the home-office with his wife, Sally Campbell. In the 12 years that they've been together there, the home's ever-evolving state has served them well. "Over the years I've gone through lots of different relationships with the house," he says. "A couple of years ago, I was ready to tear it down and start over. And at one point I thought we'd move the original section of the house and build something different here. But then we got down to thinking about what we'd actually build, and it always kind of ended up being the same as it is now," he adds, laughing, "or a lot the same."

MCNAMARA HOUSE. Hornby Island, British Columbia. Michael McNamara, architect and builder.

Sim Van der Ryn & Family

c. 1972–93

THERE ARE ENTRANCES, and then there are entrances. When Sim Van der Ryn comes into his house through the front, he pushes past a J.B. Blunk chain-saw-carved, reclaimed-redwood door and steps inside a pyramid-capped, skylit room painted to induce a spiritual transformation. An expression of Tibetan Buddhist color symbolism, the vibrant palette represents the five colors of the "rainbow body," the state of meditation just before Nirvana, in which matter begins to be transformed into pure light. The room's saffron translates to rootedness; the mint to balance; the red to life force; the white to knowledge; the blue to ascension. One weekend in 2001, two of Van der Ryn's Tibetan monk friends had painted the space this way without ever really sharing with him the deeper meaning behind their work. The monks had quietly gifted Highland House something much greater than Van der Ryn had been expecting: looking back to 1969, the year he gave up a "hilltop mansion" in Berkeley for his old cabin in the Inverness woods following the police violence toward students at Berkeley's People's Park, there was a pattern of serendipitous twists. Many had come Van der Ryn's way—Highland House was one of them.

Sim Van der Ryn has been called the "godfather of green." In the 1970s, as a UC Berkeley College of Environmental Design professor and as California State Architect, he was one of the handmade house's most effective champions. OPPOSITE: A chain-saw-carved solid-redwood door, made in '72 by his former neighbor J.B. Blunk, is the introduction to the Inverness, California, handmade house that Van der Ryn designed and built for himself.

THE AFTERMATH OF BERKELEY IN THE 1960S: FINDING A PLACE TO BE

The year 1971 marked Sim Van der Ryn's tenth consecutive year with the University of California, Berkeley's College of Environmental Design. During that period he'd also gained notoriety for the work of his private architecture practice with Sandy Hirshen. In 1967 and '68, at 32 years old, Van der Ryn had been called to Washington, DC, to brief Senator Robert Kennedy on the firm's housing and camps for California's migrant farm workers. But by 1971, instead of teaching courses on campus, as he'd always done, and otherwise maintaining a presence in town, the architect and professor was off the radar, living an hour and a half away in the tiny Marin County town of Inverness. He'd walked away from the epicenter. People's Park had pushed him over the edge. "National Guard helicopters sprayed the campus with a new type of poison gas being tested for use in Vietnam," he says. "Alameda County sheriffs armed with shotguns killed one man and wounded others. My kids ran home from school, vomiting and teary-eyed from the poison gas that had wafted into their school."

"The People's Park experience had opened my eyes to the hollowness of conventional institutional forms and their authority," says Van der Ryn. "It was time to experiment, to take some risks. I told the department, 'I'm not going to teach on campus anymore. I'm sorry.'" For two years, the professor was on leave in Inverness. He added on to his old cabin, doing the carpentry and construction himself. That self-build experience left him wanting another opportunity, however. "I'm just not a very patient carpenter," he says. "I remember the day I finished the house, I went

up on the road and looked at it and I just knew it wasn't the right location." Seeking another chance, he acquired five acres of Bishop pine forest, a prime spot situated next to a nature conservancy, and started contemplating the possibilities for a new house.

Meanwhile, one of Van der Ryn's former students, architect Jim Campe, had also left Berkeley for Inverness in '69, for the same reasons. And in the two years that had passed since, they'd stayed in touch. Soon the friends began working on a plan that might allow them to resume their rewarding work at the university while also maintaining their newly adopted back-to-the-land lifestyles in Inverness. The solution would be a Van der Ryn and Campe–created 10-week UC Berkeley course. The workshop, which they'd conduct on Van der Ryn's five acres, would teach students how to build their own houses and other structures necessary for a self-reliant community while also living off the land. It was unprecedented but they were going to present it to the head of the architecture department anyway.

In the fall semester of 1971, the University of California, Berkeley, debuted the nation's first university-level course on designing and building a handmade house: Making a Place in the Country. As Van der Ryn and Campe had planned it, three days per week a group of 15 students (about half of which ended up being women) would meet at Van der Ryn's property and learn by doing. All of the building

OPPOSITE: The original second-floor living room featuring salvaged Douglas fir poles. On the shelves, a worn copy of Paul Oliver's 1977 book *Shelter, Sign & Symbol* is flagged with Post-its. Van der Ryn made the watercolors during backpacking trips through the Sierra Nevada mountains. ABOVE RIGHT: The spiral stair to what's now the master bedroom was crafted using an old utility pole, reclaimed Douglas fir planks, and salvaged redwood wine-tank staves. RIGHT: A stained-glass window in the yoga room.

materials they'd end up needing the students would reclaim themselves, with most of it eventually coming from old chicken coops. The students' creations—in 2012, a few still stand on Van der Ryn's property—were idiosyncratic and free spirited, as if each designer-builder was thumbing his or her nose at convention, reveling in the fact that he or she wouldn't have to answer to a client, or worse yet, a building inspector.

"BUILDINGS ARE NOT OBJECTS, THEY'RE ORGANISMS." SIM VAN DER RYN

Making a Place in the Country had delayed Van der Ryn's original plan of building a house for himself and his family but, at the same time, what he'd learned from the class had put him on an entirely new path with design and construction. When, in the summer of 1972, the architect finally cleared an area near an old plywood cabin that had come with the property and started what would become Highland House, he tapped back into the course's free-spirited approach. Working primarily with Paul Kornhummel, a student from the class who'd stuck around, and riffing on a framework idea proposed by local architect Igor Sazevitch, Van der Ryn completed the first incarnation of the home in less than a year. If the expansion of his first Inverness cabin had been a letdown, here he made up for it.

The original two-and-a-half-story design, a pole barn enveloped in cedar shingles, had just the right look and feel. It harmonized with the wooded site and it paid tribute to California's old ranch vernacular. Most of the structure's 12-inch-diameter Douglas fir poles had been reclaimed. The floors,

ceilings, walls, and beams were done with newly milled cypress (Alaska yellow cedar). Van der Ryn added windows from a variety of different sources, each with its own story: The leaded glass he found in a Dumpster in Berkeley; a local artist crafted the stained glass; a half-cylinder window on the second floor was made from Plexiglas, a practice he had become interested in after visiting houses in Vermont by architect Dave Sellers [see p. 35].

Van der Ryn's neighbor, sculptor J.B. Blunk, had warned the architect that "you've got to build up if you want any sun here." To that end, only a single room, a seven-sided den, comprised the ground floor. "Originally, that was the only space we could heat, with a Franklin stove," the architect says, laughing, "so we spent most of our time there." The second level was the intended heart of the house, accommodating the living room, the master bedroom, and the bathroom with its Blunk-crafted massive solid-cypress sink. A fixed ladder gave the Van der Ryn children access to their shared hideaway/bedroom space in the third-level loft. The kitchen went into the property's old plywood cabin, a 15-foot walk away. In early 1973, the Van der Ryns were unpacking their belongings and settling into it all. Unannounced, architecture critic Allan Temko showed up and they all sat in the kitchen and had dinner, toasting the new house. In the ensuing months, there would be many more surprise visits.

OPPOSITE: More rescued natural materials were used to build the master bath. At the same time that Blunk made Van der Ryn's front door, he also made the solid-wood sink. When the building inspector came out, Van der Ryn recalls with a laugh, "The guy walked into the bathroom and said, 'This isn't legal. It has to be ceramic.' And I said, well, I'm not taking it out!"

"People would just show up here in those days," says Van der Ryn. "We had a hot tub then, and it seemed like there was always someone in it." But it was only temporary; a year later, the house would be vacant.

CLASS K AND INTO TODAY

Between 1974 and the early 2000s, the Van der Ryns occupied Highland House intermittently. Once again the architect's teaching (to this day, he's still at UC Berkeley) and design work, both of which had only become more ecologically concerned as the years went by, had him on the move. In '75, he accepted the appointment from Governor Jerry Brown to serve as California State Architect. One of Van der Ryn's great achievements in that position was Class K, a new building code conceived with the kind of owner-built houses in mind that he'd developed such a passion for while in Inverness. "The state passed Class K and, with a great deal of politicking, the coastal rural counties adopted the regulations, and many technically illegal handmade houses became legal," he says. "People no longer had to fear the dreaded red tag posted by roving building inspectors, which could lead to the demolition of their handcrafted homes, many of which were works of true beauty. I still probably get a half dozen e-mails a year from people thanking me."

Throughout these years, Highland House received substantial renovations. In the mid-1970s, Tom McCoy, another student from the Making a Place in the Country class, used a 12" x 12" salvaged piece of redwood to build the ground-floor pyramid-roofed structure (now the skylit entrance hall) that connected Highland House to its original kitchen. In the late 1970s, a craftsman who'd worked for Van der Ryn at Van der Ryn's Farallones Institute in Occidental, California, built the spiral stair that's in the living room today, again using salvaged wood. In the 1980s, Van der Ryn transformed rooms and added more. The master

bedroom became a yoga room and the children's loft was transformed into the master. The ground-floor living room became a guest room. In the early 1990s, the old kitchen was knocked down and replaced with a "Japanese-style" 1,000-square-foot kitchen/dining-area/living-area wing, the work of San Francisco Zen Center head carpenter and frequent Van der Ryn collaborator Ken Sawyer.

"WHEN WE DRIVE NATURE INSANE,
WE LOSE OUR OWN SANITY."
GREGORY BATESON

In 2005 Van der Ryn returned to Highland House, and it's been his home ever since. His latest venture, the Ecological Design Collaborative, is also based here, perhaps helping to ensure that work won't lure him away again. Since returning to the house, he's added a flagstone patio off the new wing and various water features, both the work of Lance Wyeth. A pond beside the house filters the newly improved gray-water irrigation system. The electricity is entirely dependent on solar energy. Van der Ryn might be most proud of his sprawling edible garden, however, as this is where you can expect to find him in his free time.

In the spring of 2011, Van der Ryn was hosting a few young architecture fans at home. At one point, discussion drifted to the house and Inverness's many other classic handmade houses. Van der Ryn was asked if he'd ever seen the 1973 book *Handmade Houses: A Guide to the Woodbutcher's Art*. The guest had heard about the long-out-of-print classic but hadn't yet been able to locate a copy. Ever gracious, Van der Ryn smiled and then disappeared to a bookshelf in another room. Moments later he emerged holding a well-worn copy and handed it to the guest to peruse. Five pages into it, the guest abruptly dropped the book on the kitchen table, flushed with embarrassment. She'd just discovered her faux pas: not only had Van der Ryn seen *Handmade Houses*, he'd authored the book's foreword.

HIGHLAND HOUSE. Inverness, California. Sim Van der Ryn, architect and builder, in collaboration with Paul Kornhummel, Tom McCoy, and Ken Sawyer.

Mickey Muennig

c. 1974–76

IT WAS ONE OF THOSE uniquely Big Sur nights when it seems as if every star in the galaxy is screaming for your attention, each on full fiery display—nature at its most intoxicating. Mickey Muennig had been tossing and turning in bed, restless under the full moon. At one point he rolled over, gazed up through his roof, and, with divine timing, watched two meteors blaze across the sky, their fleeting, intersecting trails momentarily forming a perfect *X*. In that epic moment from 1976, Muennig's newly completed house—a dome of native granite and redwood, 18 feet in diameter and 13 feet high, with a redwood platform bed that hung 7 feet off the ground on slender steel rods that disappeared into the glass ceiling—fulfilled a significant part of its promise. Big Sur's long-cherished summertime tradition of the outdoor bed in a garden had been effectively one-upped, reinvented for year-round, all-conditions enjoyment. An entirely new sort of Big Sur shelter, this was stargazer architecture, a habitable eye focused on outer space.

For over 13 years (and with girlfriends and their children along for the ride), architect Mickey Muennig lived in the tiny Greenhouse—his take on the then-popular dome and his celestial artistic response to the 1970s Big Sur lifestyle that he'd fallen in love with. THESE PAGES: Viewed from the outdoor bath-deck that Kas built in 1984, the Greenhouse can be seen in its jaw-dropping context. OPPOSITE: Muennig on Partington Ridge, 2010.

BOLD INDEPENDENCE

The Esalen Institute, Michael Murphy and Dick Price's human-potential-movement headquarters at the site of the old Slate's Hot Springs, was Muennig's entrée to Big Sur. At the time of his visit, the up-and-coming architect was residing in Denver, Colorado, and, as his daughter Michele Muennig recalls, on his way out of a troubled marriage. It was 1971. Drawing him to Esalen were personal-growth workshops—hands-on, frequently intense forums devoted to everything from Gestalt Practice to gardening and over which Aldous Huxley, Fritz Perlz, Ansel Adams, Timothy Leary, and even Buckminster Fuller often presided.

The Esalen experience opened the door to just what Muennig was after at the time: a way of navigating life that was different from what he'd always known—an integrated open-heart/open-mind approach. During the stay, word of his professional background spread among the workshop attendees. Having studied under Bruce Goff and Herb Greene, both of them countercultural architects known for houses that could look like an animal or an insect and cause a metamorphosis in those who call them home, the similarly eccentric Muennig was someone of special interest to Esalen's seekers. In this other-worldly setting, which right on the Esalen grounds included Carmel architect Marcel Sedletzky's recently completed spaceship-like Simkin House, Muennig fit right in. A commission to renovate a house for a fellow workshop attendee quickly materialized. Already seduced by the "God's country" that is Big Sur, Muennig needed no further incentive. He was relocating to Big Sur and striking out on his own.

SIGNATURES

"One of the aspects of this place that I loved the moment I got here is that money didn't drive *anything*," says Tim Green, who moved to Big Sur in 1974 and became Muennig's neighbor and close friend. "It just didn't drive anything. People were *living*, and they would have to make a little money to live. But, you know, money didn't drive it."

The Big Sur of the 1970s was also a culture of free expression and acceptance, a community where Muennig could find the headspace he'd been seeking to develop his work. The scene changed in the '80s, when second-home aspirants from Los Angeles and San Francisco starting showing up in droves. For Muennig, though, this was good for business. Now the exotic, frequently surrealistic design concepts that he'd been carrying around in his head for so many years could be sold to individuals with the mettle and the resources to actually build them. But Big Sur's formidable sense of place is linked to a building tradition. In Muennig's Big Sur work, that vernacular would be considered and respected, if not openly embraced. By the late 1990s, however, following the completion of several houses and the widely acclaimed resort the Post Ranch Inn, Muennig had effectively expanded the vocabulary of "the Big Sur look." At this point, a Mickey Meunnig building actually said *Big Sur*.

ICONOCLASM

After he had settled in Big Sur and worked his way into its tightly knit community, Muennig secured a small place on the Partington Ridge property of Giles Healey,

"There were never any plans," recalls Jack Stratman, who did the woodwork (including making the doors and windows). "There may have been a drawing but, really, we just winged it." The timber, all of it redwood, was reclaimed from another Muennig project on Partington Ridge, the Sam Preston House. LEFT: For the kitchen, Muennig handed Stratman a redwood plank that daughter Michele Muennig had carved and said, "Build it around this." Using tiles by their artist-neighbor Bob Nash, Michele made the backsplash mosaic.

an archaeologist, United States Navy navigation expert, and astronomer. "At Giles Healey's place, Mickey lived in the little shed off the garden," says Wendy Brooks, who met Muennig in 1973 and had a long-term relationship with him. "When I started hanging out with Mick, he already had the architect's stoop—the shoulders and neck a bit forward from working at the table. We would lure him down to Esalen for massages late at night, followed by the sulfur baths. But mostly Mickey spent endless hours alone in his studio, drawing spirals and spacing out and laying the foundation for what would become the exquisite and treasured homes of the next decade."

"Mickey loved good whiskey and fine cars, even when he was poor," adds Brooks. "A fine car on Partington Road made absolutely no sense, but then Mickey never sought to make sense. He had a fondness for woven Guatemalan shirts and sandals. Most of all, Mick wanted a piece of land, and he had it picked out."

TOWARD A NEW ARCHITECTURE

In the first edition of his 1957 book *Big Sur and the Oranges of Hieronymous Bosch*, Henry Miller published a photograph showing the general whereabouts of his own house on Partington Ridge. "One feels exposed—not only to the elements but to the sight of God," was how Miller described the scene. The picture also reveals a glimpse of the property that Muennig acquired, where the Greenhouse was eventually built. A stretch of bench land higher up the ridge from Miller's, some 900 feet above sea level, the Greenhouse's site was, save for a giant eucalyptus tree, completely exposed to the high drama of the coastline and the sky. In '74 it was his. Construction of the house would come much later.

A tree house was built first, and Muennig's daughter, San Francisco artist Michele Muennig, stayed up there. She recalls, "Things went *really* slow

back then. It was someone with a shovel, and if you were lucky a wheelbarrow." At one point, a friend of the architect arrived at the site in his Chevy Corvair. Equipped with an inverter, the Corvair powered the electric saws and other power tools needed for the Greenhouse. It all happened, the architect says, "on Big Sur time."

While the Greenhouse was being built, Muennig followed his muse, eventually landing in a new living arrangement but still on Partington Ridge. "Before Mickey finished the Greenhouse, he was living with me in the Tolerton House, a wonderful old handmade house on Partington that wrapped around the hill," recalls former girlfriend Judith McBean. She and

Muennig connected in '75, shortly after construction of the Greenhouse began.

"Mickey was always talking about how nothing should be square," McBean says, "like the floor is the only thing in a house that should be level. In the early '60s, before I came to Big Sur, I had been living around the Mediterranean, in Greece and North Africa. During that period, I came across the work of Jacques Couëlle in Sardinia [see pp. 140–147] and in the South of France, and I told Mickey about it. I must've had some photographs or a book. Mickey was really excited about Couëlle, and I was just bowled over by him. And by [Paolo] Soleri. Then Mickey built the Greenhouse, and the three of us—me, my daughter, and Mickey—managed to live there."

CONSTELLATIONS

One day, not long after Muennig, McBean, and her daughter, Natashia, settled in, a neighbor pulled up in front of the house in his Jeep. It was Giles Healey. In addition to about a dozen of his dogs and a bottle of Chartreuse, he'd brought along his theodolite. "Giles used the theodolite to align the house off the North Star," Muennig says. "We marked the spot that was true to astronomical north. We had a ceremony when we did that." With little more than a built-in bench, a glass-topped table, and "other old stuff" serving as furnishings, the interior of the finished Greenhouse was not exactly equipped for hosting parties. And under a cloudless sky it could get hot in there. But that didn't detract from the house's livability. "I got some fabric that you could hook up and create shade," remembers McBean. "When we were all a lot younger, *everything* was okay. I don't remember it being that hard. My kid had her own little niche in the place. We were used to living in Spartan places."

The Greenhouse's interior, despite the obvious limitations of its closetless 255 square feet of floor space and tiny kitchen, still imparts a feeling of utter expansiveness, one limited only by the ceiling of the sky. And from all the stone, which Muennig says he collected over time from the side of nearby Highway 1 after various mudslides freed the rocks from the mountains, comes a richly textured visual complexity and a strong protective feeling (although it makes hanging art a special challenge). Rooting the house to the vernacular of Partington Ridge and anchoring it firmly in the handmade aesthetic, though, is Muennig's choice of reclaimed-redwood bridge timbers for the bed platform, the mullion beams of the roof, and for the kitchen cabinetry, the latter featuring hand-carved ornamentation. Paying further homage to the local sense of place, Muennig's kitchen backsplash is covered with ceramic tiles by his neighbor and friend Bob Nash.

CENTEREDNESS

By the mid- to late 1980s, Muennig had found enough professional success to afford to build a much more substantial house next door to the Greenhouse, where, in 1989, he moved in. Nowadays, the Greenhouse still sees a lot of use, most often when old friends visit. "They like staying there," says Muennig. "A lot of good memories were made there." His friends agree.

"Once, years later, when I had married and begun my 'real world,'" recalls Brooks, "I was dreadfully upset and got in my VW Bug and drove to Big Sur just to hang out on the ridge with Mickey for a little while. I got there and into his arms and we talked, and then he went and got a piece of graph paper and drew a spiral on it, a big spiral, and said, 'You are hanging out here on the edge of the spiral, and it sounds like you need to move back to the center. The farther out you go in one direction, the farther out you'll go in the opposite direction. And if this is all too much, then go back closer to your core.' In architecture, yoga, life, it's all about spirals. And Mickey is the master."

THE GREENHOUSE. Big Sur, California. Mickey Muennig, architect. Ralph Burns, stonework. Jack Stratman, woodwork. Michele Muennig, cabinet carvings and tile mosaic.

As a teenager, Michele Muennig began salvaging building materials in and around Big Sur, intending to someday build a house for herself. THESE PAGES: The front elevation of her completed vision, which was built on her father's land on Partington Ridge. Designed with still more help from her father, architect Mickey Muennig, the house was built by former Partington Ridge-based carpenter Kas. RIGHT: Michele at home in San Francisco in 2011.

Michele Muennig
with Mickey Muennig

c. 1976—91

ARTIST MICHELE MUENNIG said good-bye to Big Sur's isolated beauty decades ago. But from inside her San Francisco studio, surrounded by her paintings, her glassworks, and the many other creations she's made by hand, she can indulge herself in the time-honored Sur ceremony of watching the sun slip into the Pacific. Her time now, though, is mostly devoted to art—making it and teaching it. She just had a show at a prominent gallery in the city, and other work is about to debut in Germany. Nowadays, Muennig keeps her Big Sur experience—her teenage years and a handful of episodes thereafter—filed away in the back of her mind. Decades have passed since she roamed Partington Ridge's lupine-lined trails, living, as she was at age 15, entirely on her own and out

out of a tiny ramshackle toolshed while her father, visionary architect Mickey Muennig, pursued his muse and his art, on the same mountain but very much at a distance. She's moved on and found her own way, settling into a distinctly metropolitan groove. But hidden deep in the woods atop that storied ridge in Big Sur, down a steep dirt road only passable to a vehicle equipped with four-wheel drive, Muennig left behind a piece of herself. The house conceived by that fiercely creative, self-sufficient-by-necessity 17-year-old still breathes.

INTERCEPTIONS

Here along Highway 1's dramatic meander, most of the homesites are completely out of sight. Only with a local's know-how can you find your way in. In the mid-1970s, the beginnings of Big Sur's real-estate boom, wealthy vacation-home aspirants from out of town snapped up many of the coastal properties. More often than not, these new landowners sought to build anew and the existing structures were wiped out. In those days it wasn't uncommon to find old chicken coops, barns, and other utility structures, not to mention entire preexisting houses, dismantled and stacked piece by piece in a pile at a property's roadside edge, ready to be hauled to the junkyard. (To a great extent Mickey Muennig got his career off the ground by conceiving houses for a number of these to-die-for lots.) At the same time, wherever new construction was being completed there tended to be leftovers—more perfectly good building materials that, in due course, would be trucked to the same nonsensical fate. But for a few years, starting in 1976, some of these piles were disappearing before that could happen. One by one, they were loaded into the back of a red 1959 Chevy one-ton pickup truck and taken to a certain spot on Partington Ridge for

LEFT: The lone bedroom has two sleeping areas: a loft partly supported by a utility pole and a nook that's large enough for a queen bed. The wine tank's radial sky-lit roof is built with reclaimed Douglas fir and redwood. OPPOSITE: A common local practice, a live-edge redwood-slab counter divides the dining area from the kitchen. Michele designed and made the tiles in the tinted-concrete floor to echo the colored rings that would appear when sunlight passed through the wine-bottle walls.

safekeeping. Behind the getaway-truck's wheel was a rail-thin blonde teenager who had worked out a plan with her architect father's construction crews. Whenever they came upon good materials finds up and down Highway 1, she'd get tipped off and jump in the truck. This was Michele Muennig then.

CAUTIOUS COLLABORATION

"I wanted something in between a circus tent and a nautilus shell," says Muennig, recalling the drawing she made of her original concept for the house, which was built on land owned by her father. "When I was

growing up, I was really into the circus. I had this fantasy that the circus was one day going to come through Joplin, Missouri, where we lived when I was a kid, and I would leave with them and spend the rest of my life working with them. I always had this fantasy of the circus. But it just kind of came out in other ways."

When it came to drawing, she had a natural ability. And as the daughter of Mickey Muennig, growing up she was regularly exposed to extraordinary architecture, through books and otherwise. "As a child I spent time driving across the country to see a Bruce Goff house or a Frank Lloyd Wright house, staying

with architects along the way," she says. Her strong sense of independence was also born from these experiences. "My father was always pretty self-absorbed," explains Muennig. "You know, to the point that we'd be driving cross-country and he'd be drawing some design in the condensation on the windshield."

But despite the divisions between them, Muennig still had the wisdom to see the value in reeling in her father and getting him to collaborate with her on her house. Eventually she presented him with a list of everything she had collected for its construction. "I said, 'Can you design me a place around these materials?' It was probably the most challenging thing he'd ever been asked. And he said, 'Well, I don't have a whole lot of time. If you should come up with some idea of what you want I'll help you.' Basically, he showed me how to do a working drawing. So that's what I did. I drew up a design and gave it to him. And he then drew up one that was better." The collaboration managed to acheive the unthinkable: it made inventive use of the menagerie of rescued parts.

CONCORDANCE

Where the rutted dirt road that feeds into the property concludes, there's a momentary break in the thick forest, a cleared area that doesn't stay level for long. It's partly canopied and has good southern exposure. Here, father and daughter sited their design, which their good friend Kas built. The house today reads as a riff on the more prominent imagery and themes of progressive 1970s Big Sur home design: part wine vat, part dome; all of it laid out for casual living, spontaneous entertaining, and easy indoor-outdoor flow. From the dome—it has a roof of glass panels that had originally been ordered for Mickey Muennig's Greenhouse (see pp. 186–191) but were sized incorrectly and therefore cast off—and the double-height living area, Michele Muennig gets her circus-tent atmosphere. And inside the wine-vat portion of the architecture is an intricate radial skeleton and a wrought-iron spiral stair that go a long way toward suggesting the inside of a nautilus shell. The young girl had won out.

IDIOSYNCRASIES

All of the tiles are handmade by Michele Muennig using local artist Bob Nash's kiln. Stained-glass windows crafted by her (she has two degrees in glass and has taught at the New Orleans School of Glassworks) infuse the dining area and the kitchen with luscious color. A south-facing wall in the living/dining area has a refined version of the then-popular wine-bottle wall. Muennig constructed it herself using bottles collected from her neighbors and from places such as Nepenthe restaurant. "I left them corked so they'd be insulated," she says. When the sun hits the different

colored bottles, a wide kaleidoscopic stream of light blasts onto the earth-toned tinted-concrete floor. The bedroom, which is held, loftlike, in the upper portion of the vat and overlooks the living/dining area, has a wrought-iron railing that Muennig had the fabricator bow to resemble a whale's ribs. "I thought it would give that area more space," she says. Muennig's mark is everywhere in the house.

Despite all her work, Muennig ended up residing at the house only for a matter of months. "I didn't stay in one place too long," she explains. "Partington was great back then. Someone was always throwing a party. Someone would tell stories. We would dance until late. But I was restless in Big Sur."

Today, Michele Muenning's house is the domain of a grateful tenant. It's been years since Muennig lived here, and she has no intention of moving back. For her, the building is like an artwork from her past that's gone on to find its own life—out of sight, yes, but not out of mind.

MICHELE MUENNIG HOUSE. Big Sur, California. Mickey Muennig, architect, with Michele Muennig. Jonathan "Kas" Kasparian, builder.

OPPOSITE: In 1991, Michele returned to Big Sur for a short time and built a bathing pavilion in the woods beside the house. Its cast-iron tub is enveloped by more of her mosaic work. ABOVE LEFT: A Michele Muennig bottle wall by the living room fireplace. ABOVE: The living/dining area's roof is domed using old redwood trusses that Michele acquired for $5 each. In his design, Mickey Muennig inverted them, challenging Kas to invent a construction solution. The current resident, Alana Cain, sits at the dining table.

Architect George Brook-Kothlow's own house in Carmel Valley,
California, marries the warmth and soulfulness of the agrarian
woodbutcher sensibility with the flat-roofed, nature-focused
forms of high-art Modernism—an approach that he's evolved
since the late 1960s. THESE PAGES: The garden elevation of the
three-bedroom house, where the living room unfolds to a patio
dining area. "The garden's in transition," says George, tongue
in cheek. Several astronomical water bills later, they pulled
the plug on the lawn and ceded control to the wildflowers.
OPPOSITE: Jennifer Brook-Kothlow, surrounded by her paintings,
in her home studio in 2010.

George & Jennifer Brook-Kothlow

c. 1978—80

"HOME" WAS AN 8' X 12' POT SHED— space enough for little more than a double bed but ample room to ponder how they might reduce the construction time of their house, which was going up in fits and starts only feet away. The first structure completed on the 2 and a half acres that George and Jennifer Brook-Kothlow had acquired from musician Joan Baez had been the shed. Living in it was never part of the plan, however. To minimize expenses during construction, the architect and his artist wife had given up the comforts of their rental, Baez's former house, which occupied part of the adjacent lot. By the summer of 1978, they'd spent months roughing it in those tight confines, "mice and all." The couple's two daughters, 11-year-old Marit and 16-year-old Ingrid, were similarly out of sorts, sleeping in an Airstream trailer parked next door.

In the mornings, George would step out of the pot shed and directly onto his construction site. A meeting with builder Pat Jewell would typically precede his heading off for the day to tend to other demanding in-progress work for clients such as Clint Eastwood. For her part, Jennifer would coordinate the kids' activities, then pull on a pair of work gloves and become a member of the construction crew, alternately wrapping pipes, wheelbarrowing sand into forms for the concrete work, and swinging a hammer. They were working hard and making sacrifices, and the days slipped away quickly. Then finally, Jewell had the house's walls and roof in place. The adventurous family traded one extreme for another, moving into a house that wasn't exactly done.

"At that time, we didn't even have running water," Jennifer explains, looking back with a laugh. "And when we finally did get the plumbing hooked up, months later, the girls and I held hands and danced around it. Ah, the memories are nice but it wasn't so nice when we were living it!" Like the self-built residences of so many artists, architects, designers, and builders, the Brook-Kothlow House would be a lived-in work in progress. As far as George and Jennifer are concerned, it still is today.

TURNING POINTS
AND TRANSITIONS

Get in your car at the start of Pebble Beach's 17-Mile Drive and don't stop until the end of Big Sur's Highway 1. Along the way there's a multitude of residential lots that rank among the most naturally dramatic and picturesque in all of the United States. This is the terrain, after all, that so captivated photographers Edward Weston and Ansel Adams. Since 1966, the year he departed Warren Callister Architects, subsequently striking out on his own with a commission from Claire Chappellet, George Brook-Kothlow has designed houses for some of the most prized of these locations. A few are visible from the road. Hill of the Hawk, the name given to the Chappellet project, a house for a magical 400-acre private ranch situated 1,100 feet over the ocean in Big Sur, would prove to be more than just a fortunate beginning for the then-30-year-old architect, however.

A 3,500-square-foot, three-pavilion timber-frame structure built of monumental (30-foot-long 8 x 22s) reclaimed redwood bridge timbers, large expanses of glass, and beach rock, Hill of the Hawk managed to achieve the ultimate architectural feat: it graced the site's epic sense of place. It looked *and* felt right. Among friends of the Chappellets, word about the house spread quickly. But its publication in the May 25, 1969, issue of the *Los Angeles Times Home* magazine, with color images by Morley Baer, sealed the architect's fate. Soon Brook-Kothlow had clients coming to him for houses with that same spirit and energy. In quick succession, other bridge-timber designs followed. There was Staude House (1969) and Coker Studio (1971), both in Big Sur; Kemnitz House (1974) in Carmel; and a house for Clint and Maggie Eastwood (1976) in Pebble Beach. These weren't clones of each other, however. With each new design the architect was evolving the concepts that made Hill of the Hawk special. The site, he says, was always important: "These were structures that reflected the environment."

By the late 1970s, Brook-Kothlow had been on an intimate journey with three primary materials: glass, native stone, and titanic reclaimed redwood bridge timbers. This was his palette. His houses

As throughout the house, the dining room and kitchen's 6" x 12" posts and beams were saw-sized from the 12" x 12" redwood that George had salvaged in the mid-1960s from a decommissioned Russian River railway bridge in Duncans Mills, California. None of the beams was sanded, sandblasted, or oil treated, as they wanted to retain the original texture and patina. With so much warm color inherent in the architecture, including the redwood shiplap partial-height walls, and with the radiant heat in the floors, there's no need for rugs.

celebrated honest structural expression, and with all that reclaimed wood they were inherently concerned with handcraft. The amount of finishing applied to the exposed timbers controlled the level of rusticity. Some clients wanted more of it than others. The original idea to use the salvaged bridge timbers, the defining element in the palette, came from Chappellet, Brook-Kothlow says. But he didn't need persuading. "We were all interested in reusing material," he recalls. "I was, anyway. By then, Dan Liebermann had been using it. For Claire, I went and found this bridge across the Russian River that was being taken down."

ARRIVALS

In late 1977, more than a decade after he paid $65 per thousand board feet for the 280-thousand-board-foot stash of 1908 railroad-bridge redwood that had gone into Hill of the Hawk and Coker Studio, Brook-Kothlow was once more sizing up the salvage at his Carmel Valley storage facility. There were enough of the 24-foot-long 12" x 12" timbers, he concluded, for at least another house. This one would be for himself and his family. Its construction would mark the last phase of the architect's journey with the reclaimed bridge timbers.

It's now April of 2011, 33 years after he and his wife had started on the place, and Brook-Kothlow is explaining his house's structural assembly while passing through the 64-foot-long open-air "solarium"

OPPOSITE: A guest bath with a sky-lit shower has the clean detailing that characterizes the woodwork in the house—the crude materials are handled with precision. Jennifer threw the sink and the vase in her pottery studio on the property. (The house's three bathrooms came late; for the first few years, they had only a simple shower in the garden.)

that links the three pavilions that complete its floor plan: living, dining, kitchen, office, and bath; children's bedrooms and bath; and the master suite. "The solarium was originally to be covered in glass," he adds, "but we liked it open so much that we just left it this way." It's a defining feature of the house. After all, in order to go from the master bedroom to the kitchen, for example, you must walk outside and through a part of the roof-less solarium. "You couldn't have this in the Midwest obviously," says the Minnesota-born architect. "But you can in California, on this site. If it's really pouring, we might take an umbrella." The entire residence is nestled into a southerly oriented hillside with each of its pavilions placed at a different step of the terracing, resulting in a dynamic room-to-room feel, one where the private spaces are indeed private. Throughout the interiors, skylights span the full length of the laminated redwood 2" x 4" ceilings. Clerestories and oversize custom windows and glass-panel doors add to the airiness and help make nature a constant part of the experience. With so many openings, the vistas of the surrounding Santa Lucia Mountains and the valley's verdant 10-mile meander toward Carmel Beach seem infinite. The structural framing and the exterior and interior infill, all of it redwood, is left entirely exposed, its varying caramel-and-gray patinas contrasting with the exposed steel fastening hardware of the posts and beams and the untinted-concrete floors. Radiant heat keeps the concrete warm.

"None of the walls go to the ceiling," says Jennifer, "so the heaviness of the structural elements doesn't feel heavy. Light penetrates right beneath the roof." Besides contributing to various aspects of the overall construction, the painter and potter threw and fired the sinks and chimney pots and made the bath tiles.

CONNECTIVITY

When George and Jennifer think back on their time
here, on all the memories they've made with their
kids and other family and friends, they're both reminded of their unusual connection to Joan Baez, the
one who made the house possible by selling them the
land. It's been decades since the political activist and
folk-music icon parted with her holdings in the valley.
But lately, George and Jennifer say, she's been turning up again. Baez's old house has new owners, and
George was commissioned to help with the building's
restoration and renovation. Notes from Baez to the
owners have been found at the property. She wants to
meet them. "Somehow, she just keeps coming back.
It must've been quite a nice time in her life," surmises
Jennifer. "Her heart is still here." If the house that the
Brook-Kothlows built for themselves is an indication,
it's fair to say that their hearts are here, too.

BROOK-KOTHLOW HOUSE. Carmel Valley, California.
George Brook-Kothlow, architect. Jennifer
Brook-Kothlow, interior designer and ceramist.
Pat Jewell, builder.

While certain DIY owner-builders were reimagining old redwood wine
tanks, self-trained architect Bruce Goff was finally able to realize
his own take on a vertical house. With his design for Al Struckus in
Woodland Hills, California, Goff ended up in territory uncharted by
the architecture profession—right where he'd been for the whole of
his 66-year career. THESE PAGES: The bachelor pad has one bedroom.
To gain the sculptural qualities he was after, Struckus shaped the
floor's curvature using laminated beams. The homeowner (OPPOSITE),
who was in his late 60s at the time, was fond of demonstrating the
safety of his fishing-net wall by throwing himself into it.

Al Struckus
with Bruce Goff

c. 1981

THE COLD-WATER FLAT in a rough immigrant neighborhood of Worcester, Massachusetts, where Al Struckus spent his youth, was never far away from his conscious-ness as an adult. The memories of those days from the 1920s and '30s, heavy as they were, didn't weigh him down, however. To the contrary, says his oldest child, Loxi Struckus Hagthrop, the tenement experience, a life "without a yard, without books, without art," eventually drove the high school dropout to push himself harder to reach his goals. And reach them he did, despite having a serious heart ailment to contend with. "They didn't even expect him to make it to 20," Hagthrop

says. "So what he did was that he taught himself about living a healthy lifestyle. And that is part of what allowed him to do the things he did later in life. It started him on a path. It set other things in motion. This man never gave up on anything."

IGNITION

Three thousand miles from his past, in a remote canyon of Malibu, California, Al Struckus, 50 years old and an engineer at Los Angeles–based rocket-engine company Rocketdyne, was relaxing in the comfortable house he shared with his wife and where he had raised his three children. The residence itself had "Frank Lloyd Wright" written all over it, but in fact it had come from the hand of Struckus, who had conceived and constructed the building based on one of the master's designs. "He had always wanted a Frank Lloyd Wright home," explains his daughter. "When he couldn't afford one, he bought a piece of property in Malibu and, in 1955, built a house that looked like Frank Lloyd Wright had done it. He had every one of Wright's books. We were at Taliesin West three or four times as kids. All he ever talked about was Frank Lloyd Wright. He admired Wright because he thought

OPPOSITE: Artist Kevin Marshall—who, with his wife, Ann Marshall, is the present owner—sits in the living room, the top floor of the 1,400-square-foot, four-story house. In the 1940s, Goff began using scrap glass to make natural-light chandeliers like the one seen here. The window walls were designed to screen out the "noise" of neighboring rooftops. TOP: The dining room mixes Danish Modern with Craftsman. A paper piece by Larry Samuels hangs nearby. RIGHT: The laminated mahogany front door is 6 feet wide and rotates on a central pivot. With help from architect Kendrick Kellogg, Struckus crafted the door; architect Bart Prince designed the glass.

of him as an individual." In Struckus's estimation Wright was the only architect whose work merited one's time and attention.

One day in 1972, five years after Struckus had sold the Malibu house and moved to the other side of the Santa Monica Mountains, to Woodland Hills, the architecture enthusiast had a life-changing encounter at his doctor's office. It had nothing to do with his health. While browsing the magazines in the lobby, waiting for his appointment, he opened a copy of the February issue of *Vogue* magazine and began absent-mindedly thumbing through it. By stroke of luck or, more aptly, fate, Struckus turned the page to discover a feature on the fantastical Joe Price House in Bartlesville, Oklahoma, the work of architect Bruce Goff.

Three months later Struckus was still staring at the article, mesmerized by Goff's total disregard for convention, his absolute devotion to beauty, his unbridled creativity. For the rocket engineer, the world had opened up. Then he got an idea.

LINKAGE

The painting that Struckus convinced Goff to make for him took seven months to arrive at his doorstep. The sequence of events leading up to this had begun with Struckus sending a letter to the architect's office expressing admiration and posing that while he couldn't afford to hire him to design a house, he wondered if in lieu of that the architect would take a commission for a painting. A dialogue had begun—the beginning of much bigger things to come.

When he had received the letter, "Goff thanked him and told him the approximate cost of the painting and said that he didn't know when he'd actually get

to it," says Hagthrop, who saved all the correspondence. "When my father finally got the painting, he just sat there and stared at it, completely astonished." In the letter that accompanied the finished work, Goff explained in painstaking detail how the canvas had been packed and how the packaging should be opened so as not to cause any damage to the art. He also casually noted that Struckus still had an outstanding balance of $100 on the piece.

THE PITCH

Goff had always advised his clients to "buy the site that nobody else wants." As a designer, that was where he often found the greatest inspiration—where many of his peers wouldn't bother to go. In 1979, the architect and Struckus were standing on the roof of the garage that occupied part of the recent divorcé's newly acquired, second property in Woodland Hills, California. By this point, they had developed a friendship. In front of them was the oddly situated 50-by-100-foot lot that Struckus had marked off for a new house. (The property had come with a house—in fact, it was right next to them—but Struckus had sold it to raise the money he needed to get started with Goff, meanwhile making a deal with the buyer to retain part of the lot so that he could build anew for himself. It was dicey but he'd gotten this far.) "And he looked at Goff," says Hagthrop, "and said, 'Can we build something here?'"

FULFILLMENT

"One of the things my father always told me," Hagthrop says, "was that when you find a creative person and you have trust in them, you let them create. You

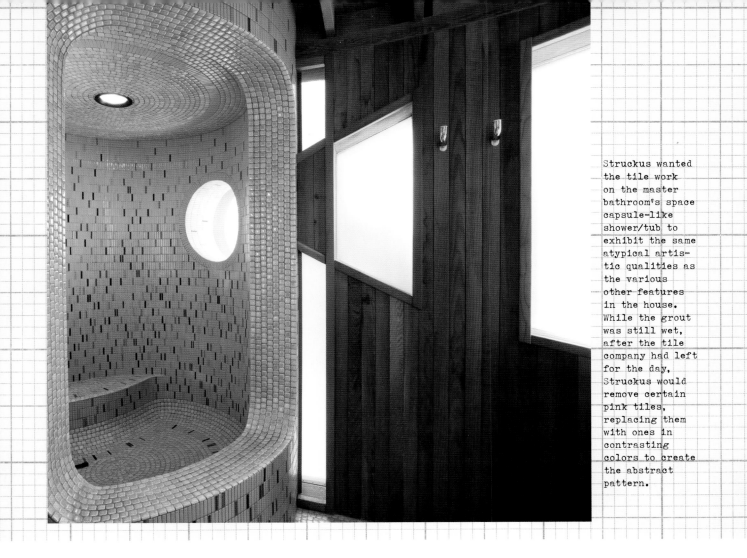

Struckus wanted the tile work on the master bathroom's space capsule-like shower/tub to exhibit the same atypical artistic qualities as the various other features in the house. While the grout was still wet, after the tile company had left for the day, Struckus would remove certain pink tiles, replacing them with ones in contrasting colors to create the abstract pattern.

don't tell them how to do it. You must take risks to achieve individuality." In February of 1981, having been otherwise occupied with work on his Pavilion for Japanese Art for the Los Angeles County Museum of Art, Goff finally revealed to Struckus what he'd created for him. As that first round of drawings was unraveled across his table, Struckus looked on intently as nearly a decade of determination and persistence was finally paying off. Goff's "Al Struckus House" was on its way to becoming a reality, and it promised to be unlike

any other house on the planet: a four-story circular tower (40 feet high and 24 feet in diameter) integrated with five equal-height cylinders positioned at intervals around its perimeter and capped with a parasol roof. At the front, each floor was given a large cyclops-like window. Windows cut in a surrealistic checkerboard pattern wrapped much of the rest of the envelope.

Inside, a free-flowing interconnectedness pervaded, as Goff cut out large serpentine-shape voids in the floors of the second and third levels, leaving one floor

OPPOSITE: At the front elevation, domed Plexiglas "lenses" sparkle in the stucco eyes, lighting the cylinder that contains the house's spiral stair. Between the rough-sawn strips of redwood resembling bark that sheath the façade, Struckus placed hundreds of tiny sparkling ceramic tiles—another layer of art and another layer of separation from the banal.

open to the other, and used centrally positioned steel arboreal arms to support the spoke-like open-beam ceilings. In one of the cylinders (the spaces where the architect placed the service functions), a spiral stair snaked its way dramatically through each level. The idiosyncrasies didn't stop, and Struckus, for his part, was awestruck. "He went into shock," says Hagthrop. "He'd never seen anything like this. He said he almost fell down!" For Goff, it must have been a familiar response.

THE AUTONOMIST

Those who visited Al Struckus in 1985 know that that was the year he finally moved out of a neighboring house and into the Goff structure. Had they arrived early enough in the morning, they would have found him stirring in his sleeping bag. Three years after starting the structure's footings but still very much in the middle of construction, Struckus, at age 68, had taken to sleeping on the floor of his yet-to-be-completed home. All along, he'd been acting as his own contractor, oftentimes doing much of the construction. Holding himself and his collaborators up to the measure of Goff's original intentions for the house, not to mention his own exacting standards, was a constant struggle, particularly in the wake of Goff's death, on August 4, 1982. "Because my father was so detailed and wanted everything done just right, he

had all kinds of people walk out on him," Hagthrop says. "He then had to learn a lot of things on his own." The house couldn't have happened any other way.

FRIENDSHIP

In the more than 10 years that it took Struckus to complete what was Bruce Goff's last house, there was one individual he could always count on to come to his rescue: Bart Prince. The New Mexico–based architect had a longstanding connection with Goff, having worked for him in 1969 while still a student at Arizona State University and, in subsequent years, associating with him on various projects. No one knew Goff's work better. "Al was in contact with me on a weekly basis while the house was being built, and of course I was out there often during construction," Prince recalls.

Goff died before all the design work and drawings were complete. Frank Purtill handled the initial working drawings and permit difficulties. Struckus worked with Prince to complete all the necessary tasks required to get the house built. Prince designed the gates and the entry-door glass, as well as several interior items that were unresolved when Goff died. "Al and I had quite an enjoyable time over the years," says Prince, "and his calls were always interesting—sometimes trying and lengthy, due to his desire for perfection. He often sent me checks for design work, but I returned them to him, suggesting he put the money into the house. I will never forget his last call, which he made only a few days before he died. He said, 'Bart, I think the house is finally finished.'"

STRUCKUS HOUSE. Woodland Hills, California. Bruce Goff, architect. Al Struckus, builder.

Daniel Liebermann has for decades stood at the forefront of ecological design, leading his clients into light-footprint houses that treat architecture and landscape architecture as a single cause, making the conventional "smart house" look ignorant. Building with rustic old wood and stone and emphasizing handcraft's natural imperfections, Liebermann uses material soulfulness to downplay the often-complicated environmental agendas of his houses. In the house for Alan Watts archivist Henry "Sandy" Jacobs, the architect was in effect mending wounds, reimagining a building ravaged by fire. THESE PAGES: The living area shows off its treelike central column, a Liebermann signature stroke. OPPOSITE: Sandy Jacobs in his attached Alaskan camper, 2010.

Henry "Sandy" Jacobs
with Daniel Liebermann

c. 1997

A HEAVY CRIMSON GLOW hung over the entire 3.5-acre property and its three residences, while in the distance a chaotic swirl of forest debris crackled and popped as it ricocheted off the trees. The atmosphere was being strangled by smoke. Standing in the midst of this surreal condition was sixty-something Dan Liebermann, one of the owners. Since daybreak, he'd been on watch while simultaneously tuned to the fire command's radio broadcast. Four days earlier, on October 1, 1995, four boys had walked away from their Mount Vision campfire after having watered and covered it with sand. But the arid October chinooks, a common wind condition this time of year, had picked up and reversed those extinguishment attempts, and now 11,000 acres of forest were gone and 2,000 firefighters were hard put to contain the blaze. The Vision Fire was raging. Liebermann's co-owner neighbor, Sandy Jacobs, had already gathered what he could and gotten out.

"I stuck around," Liebermann recalls, "because my animals were here, and I wasn't going to leave until it was serious. Finally, around three o'clock in the afternoon, I realized it was dangerous." After he'd packed his 1960 Volvo PV544 to capacity, filling it with as many household valuables as possible, he discovered one more problem: although his dog, Travis, was safely occupying the car's passenger seat, his cat, K.T., was missing. "Many of the animals around here had just disappeared, and I knew it was unlikely that I'd find her," Liebermann says. "She was a very smart, cool cat though, one who had gone through a number of her nine lives already. At the end of about 45 minutes of waiting, the smoke was thick and getting thicker. I didn't see any fire around me but I knew it was time to go. All of a sudden, there

was K.T. sitting facing the driver's side door of the car. She was smart enough to say, 'I'm ready. Let's get out of here.'" With the coyote bushes that lined his driveway now fully ablaze, Liebermann, his dog, and his cat sped away. The next time they'd set foot here, a day later, little more than the concrete foundations of their home would be left standing.

VANGUARDISTS

The orbits of Sandy Jacobs and Dan Liebermann first collided in 1960 in Mill Valley, California. Jacobs was then a widely recorded humorist and, as the host of its weekly ethnomusicology program, a public radio fixture at San Francisco's pioneering listener-supported station, KPFA. There, he had become a close confidant of fellow program-host Alan Watts, America's leading interpreter of Zen Buddhism and its comparative-religion guru. With his early proficiency with the Nagra audio recorder, Jacobs had inadvertently become Watts's archivist. Through Watts, Jacobs met his first wife, and Watts's son would go on to marry Jacobs's daughter. Liebermann, meanwhile, had settled in the Bay Area following a distinguished art-and-architecture education that included an internship with furniture designer George Nakashima and stops at Johns Hopkins University, Harvard University, the University of Colorado, and Frank Lloyd Wright's Taliesin Fellowship, where he had worked on the Guggenheim Museum. In the two years that he'd been in town, Liebermann had held designer posts with Thomas Church & Associates and Aaron Green, among other reputable firms.

But it was the work that Liebermann was doing on his own time around 1960, on an ecologically attuned little house that he himself designed and built in Mill Valley using salvaged materials, the seminal first in a series of green-minded designs, that got him noticed in the community and by Jacobs. Eventually, the radio personality and the architect forged a friendship, with the spirit of sharing being a big part of the bond.

Years later, in 1974, when Liebermann was divorcing and in need of a place to live upon returning from his eight-year relocation to Norway, Jacobs rented him a room at his Mill Valley house. In '79, after Jacobs had moved to Inverness, Liebermann, who was then residing and working in Berkeley, would periodically arrange to use Jacobs's place as a getaway. "Anybody who spent time in Berkeley eventually discovered Inverness as some magical playground to keep quiet about and enjoy," says Jacobs. Looking to do just that, Liebermann, in '90, bought into the Inverness property that Jacobs owned with his son-in-law, making his home in one of its spec houses. Now, five years on, with their colony's buildings burned to the ground, the old friends were beginning a new chapter. It was clear as to who would be the architect of it.

SEQUELS

"Sandy's building is a two-fold recycled project," says Lieberman, referring not only to the new structure's timber source—burnt Douglas fir trees were felled and milled on site—but also its incorporation of the original building's rhomboid-shaped foundation wall and the concrete bunker that had been constructed to house the Alan Watts tapes but was empty at the time of the fire. "The roof has a stepped elliptical logarithmic shell shape to it," he continues. "It's timber steps and mullions, the sort of thing I do in my regular buildings."

The Jacobs House does continue certain themes evident in all of the architect's residential works. The most prominent among them is the treelike central structural column that supports a parasol roof. Visually, the recycled-steel column with its heavy roof beams defines the free-flowing, light-filled experience of Liebermann's "arboreal architecture," and since the 1960 Mill Valley house, it's been an integral part of his trademark.

"The columnar design focuses all structure visually and technically," the architect says, "and liberates to a greater degree the external and internal walls for future growth or change. It also allows for far more adjustment, or 'flow,' with the given site's form and features. This lends, in a very important way, to the possibility of eccentricity of shape and dimension; an irregularity carefully composed or, in other words, a more subtle Organicism."

The central column lifts the ceiling structure to 16 feet, enabling multiple loft nooks within the walls-free, all-functions-within-one-space floor plan. (The living area, dining area, office, bath, and sleeping loft all share one volume.) "It's this tiny house but it's got all these very different spaces, and they all kind of flow into one another," Jacobs says. "The whole idea of rooms doesn't seem to connect very well with the reality of this place. It's a nice idea but it doesn't have much to do with a Liebermann building life."

Just beyond the front entrance, above the living area, Jacobs hung a grand-piano-shaped platform that makes for a tree house–like space. A tree trunk supports a corner of it. Adjacent the living/dining area, on top of the Watts archive's concrete bunker, is the sleeping loft that Jacobs shares with his partner, Susan "Bakoka" Hyde. Even at 86, each night Jacobs climbs a ladder to get into bed.

After moving in, Jacobs started tweaking things to personalize the spaces. In the living area, over the house's front entrance, he found a manageable-size tree trunk and some tongue-and-groove pine to build a tree house—like loft. It gets hot up there, but despite its impracticality, Jacobs explains, "guests love it, and it adds a lot aesthetically."

The Jacobs House also carries forward the Liebermann design language's rough-hewn, well-worn finishes. "Rusticity is a big part of my formula," the architect says. "All the buildings I did before I went to Norway were done with materials I got from Cleveland Wrecking. It was gorgeous stuff, and cheap. That created a whole new aesthetic in my work. I called it *shibui*. At the time, Elizabeth Gordon had done that famous [Frank Lloyd] Wright issue in *House Beautiful*. And the whole theme was the Wrightian *shibui*."

In Liebermann's used-materials palette, there's no paint, and usually no stain. "But there's a counterpoint," adds Liebermann. "Like glass and sandblasted old fir or redwood. Steel-trowel concrete, waxed. Steel that's been sandblasted and finished in linseed oil—my technique. Copper. Salvaged military-aircraft glass. I end up consciously creating a fabric, a weave of these kinds of contrasting surfaces, which has its own aesthetic." The look is industrial, but as much as it's raw, it's also seductively warm. The great variation in texture and patina draws you in.

INTEGRATORS

Right outside Sandy Jacobs's door is a trail that cuts five miles through thick new-growth forest before concluding at the beach. He's walked it innumerable times, and it's symbolic of what keeps him so enthralled here—"no signs, no garbage cans, no industry, no people. Just plants, trees, and animals." On this, the west-facing, wilderness side of the house, Jacobs has been steadily growing the living spaces created by Liebermann, both indoor and outdoor. Enveloped by his lemonarium and covered patio space is one such outgrowth: a late-1950s-model Alaskan camper. Jacobs uses it full-time as his kitchen/dining room. For both the homeowner and the architect, the quirky add-on should be read an essential feature of the architecture.

"Liebermann's building is so different from the usual dwelling," Jacobs says. "Having felt the vibe of the place, I didn't want to defile it with fried onions. I loved the white-trash, Ozzie and Harriet–aspect of the camper vibe as contrasted with the pristine, overwhelming magnificence of the kind of spaces that Dan comes up with." What sold Jacobs on the camper as a place to use on a daily basis was its ergonomics—the fact that, from one place, "you can reach the faucet, reach the stove, reach the fridge, reach the silverware, reach the dishes, reach the breakfast cereal." He and his partner get a special kick out of using it for dinner parties. It's about intimacy.

The camper, says Liebermann, "is something that Frank Lloyd Wright would never have done, but Bruce Goff thought in that direction. Like the Bavinger House and its little pods. These are things that you could remove, take in or out, or extend. Which is sort of a prefabricatory architecture. It could be a moveable, travelable, and yet integral part of your house." And they can be had for less than $1,000.

HIGHER TIMES

These days, among Jacobs's favorite pastimes is taking an outdoor bath, something he says he does all year round, no matter what. Situated next to his solarium, where he can often be found napping in the sun, and overlooking the Point Reyes National Seashore is a pair of puncheons that function as bathing tanks. At this spectacular vantage point, he's able to put his finger precisely on his total contentment here. "The experience of living in this place," Jacobs says, "fills you with a holier-than-thou attitude toward pretty much the rest of the world. I mean, I go visit at someone's house, and they can be quite affluent, with all the goodies and landscaping and everything you can think of, but this place, even though it's tiny, it appears like a palace compared to somebody's $2 million house. I look at this as my chance to play at being Henry David Thoreau. It's a Walden Pond experience."

In the troglodytic
dwellings of Savin
Couëlle, where
normal distinc-
tions between the
fine and applied
arts are blurred,
centuries-old
peasant building
traditions are
reborn. Allowing
a site's topog-
raphy to dictate
a house's form,
Couëlle brings as
little as possible
to a house's con-
ception and takes
even less away
when it's done,
relying heavily on
existent stone and
timber resources
for his materi-
als. THESE PAGES:
The sculptural
wall lighting,
the low table, the
delicate mezzanine
railing, and the
fireplace-lintel
trim is the iron-
work of François
Thevenin.

Savin Couëlle

c. 2001

THE HEALTHY CLUSTERS of juniper and strawberry trees coloring the roadside do their best to disguise the entrance path, but for Savin Couëlle, it's always easily found. Since the 1960s, the architect has been breaking away to this isolated corner of Sardinia's Costa Smeralda, to his "secret beach," for his daily afternoon swim. It's the end of November now and the Mediterranean has an off-putting chill, but the 82-year-old Couëlle doesn't hesitate. Once through the path and onto the beach, he quickly undresses, drops his clothes and towel onto the coarse pink sand, and runs into the turquoise expanse, clearly relishing every step of his ritual. Couëlle says that, in the nearly 50 years since he began contributing to Prince Karim Aga Khan IV's then-new ecologically focused "super resort" called the Costa Smeralda, this beach hasn't really changed. You won't find cigarette buts or empty plastic water bottles here. On the sand or in the sea, there's not a speck of litter. There are houses nearby but each is effectively draped in the landscape's granite outcroppings and foliage. And perhaps most surprising of all, this "secret beach," says Couëlle, is still discussed in a whisper.

In 1964, the Aga Khan was asked by a reporter to explain why he and his partners were spending hundreds of millions of dollars developing Sardinia's northwest coastline, land that Sardinians saw as good for little more than herding. "The sea here takes on particularly lovely hues, ranging from the darkest blue to the purest green," he said. "There are scores of fine, sandy beaches with not so much as a cat on them. Rugged green and gray mountains drop abruptly toward the water. A carpet of purple and yellow, and red and blue flowers perfumes the air." Today, despite the flood of tourists that impacts these shores every summer, the beauty that the Aga Khan praised so long ago remains in full bloom.

In the summer of '99, Couëlle was taking his daily swim when an Italian man recognized the celebrated architect and swam over and introduced himself. He went on to explain that he had land in the Costa Smeralda overlooking its Robert Trent Jones–designed golf course and wanted a villa for it. "And how would you like this house?" Couëlle asked his potential new client. "He just said, 'You,'" says Couëlle.

The outcome of that meeting in the sea, Villa Karim, was completed in 2001. "With this 'You,'" Couëlle remembers, "I made a house following my spirit and mood, a house that looks upon a beautiful view. It hasn't happened to me many times before—to meet a person with no aggressiveness. I liked making the house this way. You build a house for people, and I would never contemplate building a house for somebody I didn't like." The villa is one of his favorites.

CINEMATIC DEBUTS

In 1956's *Cette Sacrée Gamine (Naughty Girl)*, emerging sex symbol Brigitte Bardot, while charming her way through a thin slapstick script, glides in and out of dozens of deftly designed stage sets depicting Classical Revival–style rooms. It's not a film that's likely to be on any design buff's must-see list, but were you to happen upon it and make it to when the credits roll, surely it would take on certain new value. Listed among the film's production designers is Savin Couëlle. In the 1950s, following his architectural studies at the École Nationale Supérieure des Beaux-Arts in Paris (he was admitted at age 16), the Aix-en-Provence–born art-and-architecture prodigy ventured into the movie business. He designed parts of sets

for Jacques Becker's *Ali Baba and the Forty Thieves* (1954), where he came under the influence of noted art director Georges Wakhévitch, and Yves Allégret's *Oasis* (1955), among other pictures. Working in the same capacity, he went on to join producer Samuel Bronston's operation in Madrid, the company that in 1961 made the epics *El Cid* and *King of Kings*.

Set design work requires that you be a meticulous researcher and crafter of worlds past, present, and future. Much of Couëlle's free time in Spain was spent going deeper, roaming the countryside, "gipsylike," and studying the characteristics of its old farmhouses and other historic peasant buildings—its architecture without architects. "The castles of Castilla, the caves of Grenada with the gipsies living inside them—their life, music, habits—and the Moorish architecture in Grenada and Cordoba," he says, captivated him. Beginning in the 1960s, he would bring that same passion to the study of the vernacular architecture of Sardinia, to its Bronze Age towerlike granite structures

FAR LEFT: At the entrance hall, Couëlle reveals his palette: twisted, richly scented juniper, white ferrocement, golden beach granite, black metal (in this case, blackened copper), and sea-toned glass scraps. LEFT: He found a rock on the site that felt right, which inspired the door's design. OPPOSITE: Just inside the front door, Villa Karim makes its first impression with a view of the floor plan's rapid descent down the hillside. The master suite and guestroom are up the stairs.

called *nuraghi* and its *pinnetta*, the typical Sardinian shepherds' huts made of granite and juniper and olive poles. Aspects of each of these building types would end up converging in his houses.

NUOVE DIREZIONI

In 1963, when Couëlle began work on his first project on the Costa Smeralda, the widely published Hotel Cala di Volpe, an international team of designers, artists, and craftsmen was already busy realizing the 54-room hotel's medieval fishing village architecture. Couëlle's father, Jacques Couëlle, the building's architect, had set this in motion. But with projects outside of Sardinia requiring his attention, the elder Couëlle was no longer directly overseeing the job. "While traveling in Venice, I met my father," says Savin, "who was deeply worried because he couldn't follow the work on Sardinia for the Aga Khan. The building company was not able to understand and follow his sketches. So I came to Sardinia only to help. But as the Aga Khan loved my way to create and build and my respect for nature, he asked me to stay." At that time, many of the hotel's details were still unresolved, and so the appointment was an opportunity for Savin to apply his own well-developed artistic vision. "He took over the direction of the works—the decoration, the painting, the colors, etc.," says Eliane Aerts, one of the artists who created trompe l'oeil murals and other paintings for the hotel in the early 1960s. "His father gave him a free hand." The overwhelming success of the project set Savin on a course that would see him creating houses and other buildings for clients around the world.

The design and construction of the Hotel Cala di Volpe, an old-world melding of architecture, art, and

craft, resulted in the formation of a sublime new design vocabulary, a distinctly Mediterranean handmade look. Its salvaged-tile roofs, pastel stucco façades, Thevenin-designed iron railings and grillework, and cane-and-raffia awnings, together with sculpted white cement walls, olive trunk or tile floors, doors dressed in a patchwork of copper or bronze, twisted-juniper-pole ceilings, and cullet windows, would be copied for decades to come. In Villa Karim, there are many lively echoes of it. But, of course, here they came from the hands of one of the aesthetic's originators. It's his signature.

A NEW-MILLENNIUM CAVE

Like most of Savin Couëlle's works, Villa Karim began conventionally, with a set of standard architectural drawings. For this steep hillside overlooking the golf

course and the Mediterranean, he drew up a three-level structure with four bedrooms and three baths. The cavernous interior harnesses the site's granite boulders to its advantage, turning them into functioning parts of the living space—sofas, a hearth, walls, and room dividers. The trowelled walls and ceilings are painted bright white, enabling the strongest possible contrast between the curvaceous architecture and artful embellishments like François Thevenin's primitive-looking ironwork and the cullet windows that Couëlle himself crafted for the house. Dressed in rough-cut local granite blocks, the building keeps concealed its internal feminine figure as it grows out from the sloping landscape, gradually stepping down the hill toward the view. From the street, the house is barely visible.

Some of these features were in the blueprints. Most weren't. For this architect, the blueprint is really only a jumping-off point. It's when he's on-site, with the materials in his hands, that the building finds its form. Constantly, he improvises, tweaking the rebar according to "what the site wants." As a process, it's highly spontaneous—the exact opposite of conventional architectural practice.

"The architectural form of my houses," Couëlle says, "reaches from rock to rock, and inside I work without removing anything. What's most important is that the house and land are one—a complete whole. The land is my greatest ally because it tells me how the house will be."

All of Villa Karim's materials are locally sourced, if not taken directly from the site itself. Working with his team of Sardinian craftsmen, Couëlle's modus operandi here, as always, was "take very little in and bring even less out."

Like the post-1960 "landscape house" designs of his late father, Couëlle's houses are what he calls "basket structures"—steel rebar and wire mesh covered inside and out with sprayed-on concrete. It's a technology that he took to right away in the '60s and has never abandoned. It allows him to literally sculpt a house's spatial flow and choreograph the interplay of light and shadows and orchestrate all the sightlines. "While I am building a house I am 'in' the walls and the floors, and I completely forget about other houses and other things," he told Architectural Digest. Over the years, Couëlle has constantly elevated this handcraft-heavy building approach—the results of which produce what he's called "a luxury cave." "Every house is unique, like every person," Couëlle says. "Building it is love."

Watching Couëlle guide the book's photographer through the "most significant" aspects of Villa Karim, running his hand over the voluptuous curves of the walls as if they were body parts of a woman of his desire, it's clear that the architect hasn't lost any of his youthful vigor. When it comes to his art, he's still the 20-something bon vivant who used to haunt the "jazz caves" of the Saint-Germaine-des-Prés with the likes of novelist Boris Vian and poet Jacques Prevert. For Couëlle, the night is still young.

VILLA KARIM. Sardinia, Italy. Savin Couëlle, architect. François Thevenin, ironwork,

Greg &
Valmarie Zorila
with Dave Sellers

c. 2008

THE FIREWORKS WERE RIGHT ON CUE. Within moments of learning that they'd been selected as winners of the bid on the Wilmington property, Greg and Valmarie Zorila emerged from the house that would soon be theirs. As they gazed up from the edge of Lake Raponda they saw a rainbow bridging its spring-fed, 1¼-mile reach. A stronger prediction of good things to come for them here in Vermont, the New Yorkers (naturally) concluded, wasn't possible. That they'd emerged on top in the contentious wrangling that had marked the bidding process now seemed more than mere luck. Nature had weighed in; this was meant to be.

Driving out of the woods of Wilmington and onto the highway back to Manhattan later that day, the couple reveled in their excitement as they exchanged ideas for replacing the house, an awkwardly expanded, run-down late-1930s fishing cabin, with something that would be fitting not just for them but also for the historically significant lakefront community. This was

Dave Sellers's relationship with the handmade house now spans five decades. In the early 1980s, having fully explored the potential of plywood and found materials, he started to rethink the design vocabulary. For Sellers, the distinctly handcrafted Adirondack style had an undeniable compatibility that also lent itself to the landscape of Vermont. By the end of the decade he was merging the two aesthetics—handmade and Adirondack—and finding new craftsmanship potential in both. THESE PAGES: The lakefront side of Sellers's Zorila House, with the entrance at left and the roof of the recycled original 1930s fishing cabin projecting at far right. LEFT: Sellers in Vermont, 2010.

the lake where former presidents Rutherford Hayes and Teddy Roosevelt used to vacation, after all, and the Crafts Inn, the 1898 hotel by architect Stanford White, is nearby. While the old fishing cabin was in rough shape, the lakefront site with its southern exposure radiated potential. In the coming months, they concluded, they'd start assembling a team of architects and builders to help realize their intentions for it. They couldn't wait to get started.

ROADBLOCKS AND RECONNECTIONS

One morning in January of 2005, the Zorilas were weekending at the cabin, struggling to stay warm inside a leaky building while a snowy wind whipped across the frozen lake. Greg was seated in the living room, flipping through the channels on the TV. Seven years had passed since the Zorilas had acquired the place, and yet none of their aims for the cabin had been carried forward. Once they'd gotten into the process, they were promptly blindsided by the fact that their parcel's odd boundaries—at less than half an acre, it abutted the lake's edge on one side and overlapped a village road on the other—put them in obstruction of the right-of-way. The parcel and the fishing cabin predated local zoning laws, and now technically any new construction on that footprint would, by default, be in violation of setback regulations. Town officials had shut down the Zorilas, even with local architects at their side, at practically every turn. By this point, they'd almost given up.

OPPOSITE: As with any good front entrance, a palpable energy materializes upon entering this house. Here, using only trees, Sellers amplifies and prolongs the thrill of the experience.

Then Greg landed on the right channel. A long-prominent Vermont architect and builder, one of the pioneers of America's design-build movement, Dave Sellers was on a local TV station talking about his latest work. In 1999, right after acquiring their Vermont property, Valmarie had contacted Sellers about designing a house for them there. She'd seen a Dave Sellers lakefront house in *Architectural Digest*, and his environmentally focused design philosophy spoke to her. But at that stage the couple's resources weren't in place to make a deal, and so both parties had moved on. The Zorilas' circumstances had since improved, however, and as Greg watched Sellers on television he realized what their next move had to be.

"I just decided at that moment to call him again," says Greg. "We got the impression, because of the way he was attired and the kinds of connections he had with Vermont, that he would be able to convince the review board and the people around our town who wouldn't let us do anything for all those years. We finally decided that if anyone could get it done it was Dave Sellers."

SEEING THE FOREST FOR THE TREES

In August of 2005, Sellers & Company's Chris Dale was in a 150-acre logging area a mile from the Zorila property, carefully inspecting and tagging red maple, sugar maple, ash, and birch to be felled for the firm's latest project, something Sellers had taken to calling Fork View Lodge. What had eluded the Zorilas and their representation for the last seven years had taken Sellers and his team four months to secure. The Town of Wilmington's Development Review Board was now

on board. Finally, the rundown cabin was coming down. In its place would go the kind of house the couple had talked about since the day they learned their bid had been accepted.

"There was one really savvy person on the planning commission who understood what we wanted to do," recalls Sellers. "I said to the review board, 'We want to bring a lakeside historic house into current times while respecting what was there in the beginning.'" Sellers wanted to save the old fishing-camp-house portion, now only a room, and take down the remodeled parts, replacing them with new rooms bearing that same fishing-camp flavor. "And it had this tacky little boat-house that was being used as a garage. I proposed that we would take that out and add that square footage onto the main house," reducing the number of buildings at the edge of the lake while at the same time enlarging the house. The town bought into it.

The town review board also saw the wisdom in the Adirondack Great Camp boathouse–inspired design that Sellers presented to them, progressive though it was. Never before had they been asked to consider a set of drawings that depicted bark-covered trees with branches as an integral, structural part of a house's living space. Sellers's convincing lakeside

elevation, perhaps the most anticipated aspect of the design for board members, suggested a two-story building envelope that would appear to be constructed not on top of preexisting water's-edge tree growth but respectfully *around* it. And the 1930s portion of the original cabin, an exposed-structure room with peeled-log rafters that would become the living room of the new two-bedroom, one-bath floor plan, was seamlessly integrated. "It looks like a single idea," the architect says of the whole, "even though buried within it is this old room."

OPPOSITE: Inside, the procession of trunks continues. Sellers dictated that each tree be cut at its roots so that the root flare—"a sense of grounding"—could be visible in the finished construction. Underscoring that idea, the flares are surrounded with rocks that builder Chris Dale found in a stream running through their timber source. The custom cherry cabinets have Vermont soapstone countertops. Everything's been hand-notched into the trees. RIGHT: The pine stair treads are leftover pieces from cutting the 6" x 12" live-edge beams.

THE NATURE OF IMPROVISATION

Because Sellers's office operates on the premise that what the architect designs, the architect also builds, he and his team can and usually do improvise freely while a job is in progress, always aiming to exploit the full potential of a project's attributes using their own hands. It's an unpredictable process, one that can add considerably to the time required to finish. Artistry takes precedence over most other concerns. "When Greg and Valmarie came up to our office and said they had this old house on the edge of this lake and

wanted to do something special with it," says Sellers, "I told them, you know, if you want something *really* special and artistic and handcrafted, I'd love to do it. Long ago, I'd said that I'm restricting myself only to people that, one, I like and, two, have the interest in the best I can *possibly* do. And in that case, I don't even care what the budget is. There's only a certain amount of buildings that you can do in your lifetime."

After the Zorilas had made their pitch to the architect at his Warren, Vermont, office, Sellers took the couple on a tour of various houses he'd completed nearby, to give them some sense of where he might go creatively on their behalf. Among the buildings they saw was a signature Sellers tree design, an example of what they ultimately got but done on a much larger scale. "When I saw it," says Valmarie, "I said, 'Oh, Dave, this looks like God put it here.'"

"In our house," Greg adds, "we didn't imagine that there was going to be that level of detail. I don't think we imagined any of it. I think we thought it was going to be many steps below the house he showed us that had trees in it. For our project, we expected that he was going to cut back. He didn't."

THE PERSONALITY OF A HOUSE

On June 1, 2008, three years after Sellers made his case to the planning board, the Zorilas hosted a party, a "kickoff," at their newly completed house at Lake Raponda. The gathering wasn't for friends and family but instead for all those who'd devoted their talents to making the house possible. Sellers arrived with an old boat lit up like a parade float and had a camera crew in tow. Sellers & Company's Chris Dale also showed up. As much as any contributor, Dale was deserving of

OPPOSITE: The original fishing cabin, now the living room, has a typically monumental Sellers fireplace. Rocks gathered from the site splay up into the concrete formwork, "giving it some geometry," which is topped by a chimney surfaced with blackboard slate that they salvaged from an old Vermont schoolhouse. Sellers explains, recalling his thinking, "Let's take it from the garbage dump, honor it, and put it into this house." RIGHT: More reclaimed blackboard slate was used in the shower, each piece fastened with "nice screws and washers," highlighting the construction.

a toast. As soon as the building's plumbing had been roughed out, the then-27-year-old Yale Architecture School graduate had moved into the house in order to complete the construction and finishwork—the Sellers way. Dale lived there for a year, long enough to experience how their efforts responded to the changing seasons, long enough to see the trees dry out and change.

"For three years, I slept, ate, and drank this job," Dale says. "When I talk about this house, I always talk about how many elements are touching, or are involved with, the trees. You see window glass going into the trees, and the wall material, and the counter tops, and the flooring. Every one of those instances requires custom work. It's just chisel work, really, or small chain-saw work. But for me, it felt like the whole place was handcrafted. It was true design-build. While the trees were going up and while the timber framing was happening, and all the way through the process, it felt like working on a big found-object sculpture."

While the economic crash of 2008 slowed the Zorila's efforts to personalize the house's interiors to their liking, it never stopped them from taking time out from their lives in New York to come stay. There were other rainbows over the lake.

RESOLUTION

Today, the couple is making up for lost time, finalizing the furnishings and the art and the mementos and otherwise making the house a home. "It's been three years since the house was finished," Valmarie says, "and I can still come here and look in awe at what they did. At the beginning, Dave had told me, 'You'll see the lake's reflection on the ceiling.' And I see that now."

FORK VIEW LODGE. Wilmington, Vermont. Sellers & Company, architect and builder.

Bibliography

Addis, Bill. *Building with Reclaimed Components and Materials: A Design Handbook for Reuse and Recycling.* London: Earthscan, 2006.

Agnew, Eleanor. *Back from the Land: How Young Americans Went to Nature in the 1970s, and Why they Came Back.* Chicago: Ivan R. Dee, 2004.

Alinder, Jim, and Lyndon, Donlyn. *The Sea Ranch.* New York: Princeton Architectural Press, 2004.

Apostol, Jane. *El Alisal: Where History Lingers.* Los Angeles: Historical Society of Southern California, 1994.

Architectural Digest, Winter 1970.

Ashton, Dore. *Noguchi: East and West.* New York: Knopf, 1992.

Atkins, Guy. *Asger Jorn: The Final Years, 1965–1973.* Copenhagen: Borgen, 1980.

Ballantine, David, and Haney, Robert. *Woodstock Handmade Houses.* New York: Random House, 1974.

Boericke, Art, and Shapiro, Barry. *Handmade Homes: The Natural Way to Build Houses.* New York: Delacorte Press, 1981.

———. *Handmade Houses: A Guide to the Woodbutcher's Art.* San Francisco: Scrimshaw Press, 1973.

———. *The Craftsman Builder.* New York: Simon & Schuster, 1977.

Brady, Mildred Edie. "The New Cult of Sex and Anarchy," *Harper's Magazine,* April 1947.

Brower, David, ed. *Not Man Apart: Photographs of the Big Sur Coast.* San Francisco: Sierra Club, 1965.

Busher, Dick, and Martin, Harry. *Contemporary Homes of the Pacific Northwest.* Seattle: Madrona Publishers, 1980.

Cabanne, Pierre. "Keeping Cave: The Cave Dwellings of Jacques Couëlle," *Réalités,* (October 1969): 68–71.

Cahan, Richard, and Williams, Michael. *Edgar Miller and the Handmade Home.* Chicago: CityFiles Press, 2009.

Cardwell, Kenneth H. *Bernard Maybeck: Artisan, Architect, Artist.* Salt Lake City: Peregrine Smith Books, 1977.

Carleton, Dr. Don E. (interviewer). "An Interview with Mr. Elmer W. 'Tony' Staude," (2005–06): http://www.andersoncanyon.com/history.php.

Carroll, Peter N. *It Seemed Like Nothing Happened: The Tragedy and Promise of America in the 1970s.* New York: Holt, 1982.

Carver Jr, Norman F. *Japanese Folkhouses.* Kalamazoo: Documan Press, 1984.

Clark, Hilary. "Visit to Hilary's Home," *The Vancouver Sun,* Homes section, April 14, 1972.

Commoner, Barry. *The Closing Circle: Nature, Man, and Technology.* New York: Knopf, 1971.

Conaway, James. "Big Sur's California Dreamin'," *Smithsonian,* May 2009.

Cook, Adrian. *Villas in Sardinia: Savin Couëlle.* Canale: Gianni Mussotto, 1982.

Cook, Jeffrey. *Seeking Structure from Nature: The Organic Architecture of Hungary.* Basel: Birkhäuser, 1996.

Crandall, Chuck. *They Chose to Be Different: Unusual California Homes.* San Francisco: Chronicle Books, 1972.

Day, Christopher. *Places of the Soul: Architecture and Environmental Design as a Healing Art.* London: Elsevier, 2002.

De Angulo, Gui. *The Old Coyote of Big Sur: The Life of Jaime de Angulo.* Berkeley: Stonegarden Press, 1995.

De Long, David G. *Bruce Goff: Toward Absolute Architecture.* Cambridge: The MIT Press, 1988.

Discoe, Paul, with Quinn, Alexandra. *Zen Architecture: The Building Process as Practice.* Layton: Gibbs Smith, 2008.

Downs, Barry. *The Poetics of West Coast Modernism in West Vancouver.* Vancouver: West Vancouver Cultural Services, 2005.

Ebert, Wolfgang M. *Home Sweet Dome.* Frankfurt: Verlag Dieter Fricke, 1978.

Editors of *AD.* "Mickey Muennig/Foulke Residence, Big Sur," *Architectural Design,* Nov/Dec 1993.

Editors of *Life.* "Ideas in Houses: Not a Home but a Happening," *Life,* March 24, 1967.

Editors, "Houses at Castellaras-Le-Neuf: The Versatility of Concrete Allows for Creativity and Individualism," *Concrete Construction,* November 1971.

Ennis, Thomas W. "Aga Khan's Brain Child in Mediterranean Is Growing Up," *The New York Times,* July 16, 1967.

Fitzpatrick-Grimm, Elayne Waring. "Bob Nash...," *The Big Sur Gazette,* March 1979.

Fiz, Simon Marchan, and Martinez de Albornoz, Pedro. *Fundacion Cesar Manrique, Lanzarote.* Stuttgart: Edition Axel Menges, 2007.

Frum, David. *How We Got Here: The 70's, the Decade that Brought You Modern Life—for Better or Worse.* New York: Basic Books, 2000.

Glueck, Grace. "A Happy Marriage: In Riviera Houses, Art Weds Architecture," *The New York Times,* June 21, 1964.

Gomez Aguilera, Fernando. *Cesar Manrique: In His Own Words.* Lanzarote: Fundacion Cesar Manrique, 1995.

Goodman, Judith, ed. *Big Sur Women.* Big Sur: Big Sur Women Press, 1985.

Greene, Betty Patchin. "Historic Houses: Charles Greene," *Architectural Digest,* (May 1989): 92–108.

Gregor, Alison. "Junkyard Architecture," *The New York Times,* December 16, 2010.

Harrington, Mary. "The Legend of Sam Trotter, Big Sur," *The Big Sur Gazette,* October 1979.

Helliwell, Bo, and McNamara, Michael (contribs.). "Handbuilt Hornby," *Architectural Design,* vol. 48, no. 7, 1978.

Historic American Buildings Survey, "Deetjen's Big Sur Inn," HABS No. CA-2611. Washington, DC: Library of Congress, 1995.

Hopkins, Heidi, ed. *These Are My Flowers: Raising a Family on the Big Sur Coast: Letters of Nancy Hopkins*. Big Sur: Hopkins, 2007.

Hopkins, Jerry. "Big Sur," *Rolling Stone*, no. 44, October 18, 1969.

Huxtable, Ada Louise. "Art Houses Glow— At $160,000 Each," *The New York Times*, October 30, 1965.

Iovine, Julie V., and Merrill, Todd, eds. *Modern Americana*. New York: Rizzoli, 2008.

Jacob, Jeffrey. *New Pioneers: The Back-to-the-Land Movement and the Search for a Sustainable Future*. University Park: The Pennsylvania State University Press, 1997.

Jaffé, Aniela, ed. *Memories, Dreams, Reflections by C.G. Jung*. New York: Random House, 1961.

Jeffers, Donnan Call. *The Building of Tor House*. Covelo: The Yolla Bolly Press, 1993.

Johnson, Eugene J., ed. *Charles Moore: Buildings and Projects, 1949–1986*. New York: Rizzoli, 1986.

Joly, Greg. *Almost Utopia: The Residents and Radicals of Pikes Falls, Vermont, 1950*. Barre: Vermont Historical Society, 2008.

Jones, Michael Owen. Book Review: *Handmade Houses: A Guide to the Woodbutcher's Art*, in *Western Folklore*, Vol. 34, No. 2 (Apr., 1975), 158–60.

Jorn, Asger. *Asger Jorn*. New York: The Solomon R. Guggenheim Museum, 1982.

Kahn, Lloyd, ed. *Shelter*. Bolinas: Shelter Publications, 1973.

Kahn, Lloyd. *Builders of the Pacific Coast*. Bolinas: Shelter Publications, 2008.

———. *Home Work: Handbuilt Shelter*. Bolinas: Shelter Publications, 2004.

Karman, James, ed. *The Collected Letters of Robinson Jeffers, with Selected Letters of Una Jeffers, Vol. I, 1890–1930*. Stanford: Stanford University Press, 2009.

Kempner, Mary Jean. "Young Architects in the Spotlight," *House Beautiful*, July 1966.

Kern, Ken. *The Owner-Built Home*. Oakhurst: Ken Kern Drafting, 1972.

Kiss, Zoltan S. *Without a Blueprint: Surviving in a Changing World*. West Vancouver: Sandor Press, 2005.

Knight, Pamela. "The Aga Khan Runs a Company Town," *Sports Illustrated*, (May 13, 1968): http://sportsillustrated.cnn.com/vault/article/magazine/MAG1081159/index.html.

Lear, Linda. *Rachel Carson: Witness for Nature*. New York: Holt, 1997.

Liebermann, Daniel. "Ecological Architecture and Fractality of Spatial Perception," *L'architettura*, April 1993.

———. "The Knut Knutsen Cottage in Portor," *Arne Korsmo – Knut Knutsen: Due Maestri del Nord*. Rome: Officina Edizioni, 1999.

Littell, Robert. "Castellaras—Where All the Houses Bear One Man's Imprint," *The New York Times*, January 16, 1972.

Longstreth, Richard. *On the Edge of the World: Four Architects in San Francisco at the Turn of the Century*. Berkeley: University of California Press, 1983.

Luigi, Gilbert. *Jacques Couëlle: Parenthese Architecturale*. Belgium: Solédi – Liège, 1982.

Lundy, Susan. "New Angles: Three Generations of Building Merge in Scott Point Addition," *Aqua* (Fall 2005): 20–22.

MacMasters, Dan. "A Sculptor's House," *Los Angeles Times*, Home Section, March 24, 1968.

MacMasters, Dan. "A Visit to the Carmel Country," *Los Angeles Times*, Home magazine, May 25, 1969.

Mann, Henry Yorke. *Architecture: Part of the God Dance*. Oliver, B.C.: Manndala Publication, 1996.

McGarry, T.W. "Working Around the House, He's Building a 'Cyclops Silo,'" *Los Angeles Times*, August 28, 1983.

McKinley, Cameron Curtis. "Sur House: Bucolic Calm on California's Northern Coast," *Architectural Digest* (February 1982): 99–104.

Miller, Henry. *Big Sur and the Oranges of Hieronymus Bosch*. New York: New Directions Books, 1957.

Miller, Timothy. "The Roots of the 1960s Communal Revival," *American Studies*, vol. 33, no. 2, 1992.

Mooring, Stephen, and Sergeant, John, eds. *AD Profiles 16: Bruce Goff*. London: Architectural Design, 1978.

Morris, Stephen. "The Prickly Mountain Gang," *Vermont Sunday Magazine*, October 9, 2005.

Morton, David. "Organic Architecture at Goddard College," *Progressive Architecture*, November 1971.

Mudford, Grant (photographer), and Webb, Michael. "The Ultimate Goff: A Maverick Architect's Towering Last Stand," *L.A. Style*, May 1992.

Nash, Bob. *On My Way: Fragments of My Life as an Artist*. Carmel: Sunflower Ink, 1996.

Nearing, Helen. *Living the Good Life*. New York: Galahad Books, 1954.

Newman, Morris. "Focus: Big Sur, Calif.; An Environmentally Correct Resort Hotel," *The New York Times*, April 28, 1991.

Noguchi, Isamu. *Noguchi: A Sculptor's World*. New York: Harper & Row, 1968.

Norman, Jeff. *Big Sur*. Charleston: Arcadia, 2004.

Oliver, Paul, ed. *Shelter, Sign & Symbol*. Woodstock: The Overlook Press, 1977.

Post, Emily. *The Personality of a House: The Blue Book of Home Charm*. New York: Funk & Wagnalls, 1930.

Progressive Architecture, June 1992.

Progressive Architecture, May 1966.

Ragon, Michel. "Jacques Couëlle," Cimaise, No. 103 (Aug., Sept., Oct. 1971).

Rayner, Anne Patricia. "Everything Becomes Island: Gulf Islands Writing and the Construction of Region." PhD diss., University of British Columbia, 1995.

Reesman, Bryan. "The House that Trash Built," *American Way* (November 15, 2009): 66–72.

Resler, Nancy. *Barbara Spring: A World of Their Own*. Davis: John Natsoulas Press, 2006.

Ress, Paul Evan. "Prince Karim Aga Khan," *Sports Illustrated*, (August 10, 1964): http://sportsillustrated.cnn.com/vault/article/magazine/MAG1076226/index/index.html.

Reynolds, Christopher. "A Dream Rebuilt," *Los Angeles Times*, September 6, 2007.

———. "A Muse for the Masses: Free Spirit James Hubbell," *Los Angeles Times*, December 1, 2002.

Rigan, Otto (essay contrib.). *James Hubbell*. Oceanside: Oceanside Museum of Art, 1998.

Rowe, Richard. "Bruce Goff in L.A.," *Society of Architectural Historians/ Southern California Chapter Review*, Spring/Summer 1983.

Rudofsky, Bernard. *Architecture without Architects: A Short Introduction to Non-Pedigreed Architecture*. New York: The Museum of Modern Art, 1964.

Sagan, Danny (contrib.). *Architectural Improvisation: A History of Vermont's Design/Build Movement, 1964–1977*. Burlington: University of Vermont Press, 2008.

Seavey, Kent. *Carmel: A History in Architecture*. Charleston: Arcadia, 2007.

Snyder, Robert, ed. *Buckminster Fuller: An Autobiographical Monologue/Scenario*. New York: St. Martin's Press, 1980.

Special to *The New York Times*, "2 Architects Put Plans Into Action; Turn Builders as They Test Ideas in Vermont Hills; Way-Out House Is Built Way Up," *The New York Times*, January 30, 1966.

Starr, Kevin. *California: A History*. New York: The Modern Library, 2007.

Stern, Sol. "Canyon: A Troubled Paradise," *Ramparts*, vol. 8, no. 5, (November 1969): 22–28.

Stone, Robert. *Earth Days* (Boston: WGBH Educational Foundation and Robert Stone Productions, 2010). Documentary film.

Time Magazine Archive, "Art: House in Big Sur," *Time* (December 28, 1959): http://www.time.com/time/magazine/article/0,9171,811614,00.html.

———, "The House: Village of Foetuses," *Time* (Nov. 22, 1963): http://www.time.com/time/magazine/article/0,9171,898030,00.html.

Treib, Marc, ed. *An Everyday Modernism: The Houses of William Wurster*. Berkeley: University of California Press, 1995.

United States Patent Office, No. 2,414,094, Jan. 14, 1947. "Building Framework," Couëlle, Jacques.

Van der Ryn, Sim. *Design for Life: The Architecture of Sim Van der Ryn*. Salt Lake City: Gibbs Smith, Publisher, 2005.

Van der Zee, John. *Canyon: The Story of the Last Rustic Community in Metropolitan America*. New York: Harcourt Brace Jovanovich, 1971.

Van Hensbergen, Gijs. *Gaudi*. New York: HarperCollins, 2001.

Welch, Philip B. *Goff on Goff: Conversations and Lectures*. Norman: University of Oklahoma Press, 1996.

Weygers, Alexander, and Weygers, Marian. *Sculpture, Form and Philosophy: The Notebooks of Alexander G. Weygers*. Monterey: Cypress Press, 2001.

Whole Earth Catalog, Fall 1969.

Williams, Anabelle, ed. *Handmade Lives: A Collective Memoir*. San Francisco: Firefall, 2002.

Williams, Christopher, and Williams, Charlotte. *Craftsmen of Necessity*. New York: Vintage Books, 1974.

Worster, Donald. *A Passion for Nature: The Life of John Muir*. New York: Oxford, 2008.

Zwack, Anne Marshall. "Shoppers World; Earthy Ceramics in Sardinian Style," *The New York Times*, June 19, 1988.

Index

For my mother, Diane, and in tribute to the memory of Big Sur, California, wood sculptor and handmade-house lover Barbara E. Spring (February 16, 1917 to June 28, 2011).

Along with everyone mentioned heretofore in the text, I want to call out the following for their help with *Handmade Houses*.

Al Weber, Al Weber Photography, Carmel, CA

Alan Berolzheimer, Vermont Historical Society

Alessandro Jelmoni

Alex Vertikoff, Alexander Vertikoff Photography, Tijeras, NM

Allan Linnemann

Ami Kirby, Topanga Historical Society, Topanga, CA

Ana Todd

Andreas Jung

Andreas Putsch

Anita Alan, author of *Big Sur Inn: The Deetjen Legacy*

Annie Weedon

Are Carlsen, Photographer Are Carlsen, Oslo, Norway

Ariel van Zandweghe, The Historical Society of Southern California, Pasadena, CA

Barbara Moon-Batista, Batista Moon Studio, Monterey, CA

Barry Downs, Barry Downs Architect, West Vancouver, B.C.

Bart Prince, Bart Prince Architect, Albuquerque, NM

Bill Behr

Bruno Blunk

Candy Barr, Candy Barr Artist, Warren, VT

Catherine Bengtson

Celia Sanborn

Christian Nimmo

Christian Prati, Serenissima Cir Industrie Ceramiche S.p.A., Italy

Christiana Wyly

Christopher and Susan Williams

Courtney Campbell

Dan Garbutt and clan

Dan Kinnard & Eloise Lau

Daniel Dole, Daniel Dole Artist Blacksmith, Berkeley, CA

Daniel Loewy

Darlene Palola

Dave Brubaker

Dave Sellers, Sellers & Company, Warren, VT

David Hastings and Sara Morris

David Nelson, Esalen Institute, Big Sur, CA

Dean Kaufman, Dean Kaufman Photographer, New York, NY

Diane Bohl

Diane Olsen Garbutt

Diane Wood

Donald M. Davis

Ed Shure, Timmerhus Log & Timber Structures, Boulder, CO

Ed Stiles, Ed Stiles Custom Wood Design/Build, Mill Valley, CA

Ehren Woyte

Elia Haworth, Bolinas Museum, Bolinas, CA

Elisabeth Tostrup, The Oslo School of Architecture and Design, Oslo, Norway

Eveline Heath and Pamela Heath

Fabio, Dolce Vita Hotel, Arzachena, Italy

Fernando Gomez Aguilera, Fundacion Cesar Manrique, Canary Islands, Spain

Fernando Ruiz, Fundacion Cesar Manrique, Canary Islands, Spain

The Getty Research Institute Library staff

Giancarlo Gardin, Giancarlo Gardin Architecture & Garden Photography, Italy

Giorgio Romani, Serenissima CIR Industrie Ceramiche S.p.A., Italy

Grant Mudford

Greg Joly

Helen Morgenrath

Jali Morgenrath

Jay Abbott and Cliff Clark

Jay Pridmore

Jennifer Bastian

Jim Simons, Vintage Redwood Company, Visalia, CA

John H.B. Peden, John Peden Photo, New York, NY

John Witzig

Juliette Bellocq, Handbuilt Studio, Los Angeles, CA

Kaya Westling

Kenneth Breisch, University of Southern California School of Architecture

Kyle Bergman, Bergman Design Team, Warren, VT

Larry Zgoda, Larry Zgoda Studio, Chicago, IL

Lloyd Kahn, Shelter Publications, Bolinas, CA

Lucia Curotti

Lyn Saberg

Magnus Toren

Maria Csaszni Rygh

Mark Boone, London Boone, Los Angeles, CA

Mark Watts

Mark Welsh, Carter & Cunningham, New York, NY

Mary Trotter, Big Sur Historical Society, Big Sur, CA

Marylu Toren

Michael Trotter

Michael Worthington, Counterspace, Los Angeles, CA

Mike Salisbury

Paola Brandano

Paolo Costanzi, Covermedia

Patricia Cievl

Pedro Martinez de Albornoz

Radek Kurzaj, Radek Kurzaj Photographer, Szczecin, Poland

Richard W. Moore, Richard Moore Construction, Killington, VT

Robert Asarisi

Rosemary Brennan

Sallie Parker Middleton

Sam Wyly

Sara Ball, Pilchuck Glass School, Seattle, WA

Sarah Healey

Sterling Doughty

Steve Wolf

Steven M.L. Aronson

Sylvia Trotter-Anderson, researcher extraordinaire and the author of a forthcoming book on legendary Big Sur figure Sam Trotter

Thomas Namey, Namey Design Studios, Knoxville, TN

Tim Biggins

Toby Rowland-Jones

Tom Birmingham, Nepenthe restaurant, Big Sur, CA

Tom Hennesey

Trish VanderBeke

Vince and Ripple Huth, The Robinson Jeffers Tor House Foundation, Carmel, CA

Wayne Ngan, Wayne Ngan Artist, Hornby Island, B.C.

I also want to thank my literary agent and old friend, Ryan Harbage, for his guidance and consistency through all the challenges we faced while making the book; Rizzoli senior editor Dung Ngo for believing in our original proposal and, later on, helping us stay on track; copyeditor Elisabeth Smith for finding the fine line between doing too much and too little; and Lynne Yeamans, the book's graphic designer, for recognizing and tapping into the spirit of the content. In the two years since we began (formally) working on the book, Allison Power, my editor, stayed loyal to it, through thick and thin, and, besides delivering us to the finish line, found ways to make the book substantially better. Rizzoli's publisher, Charles Miers, green-lighted our work based on a promise I made. (This book was made from scratch.) At a time when more and more U.S.-based illustrated-book publishers are minimizing their commitments to architecture and design by acquiring the North American rights to pre-made generic surveys originally intended for overseas markets, or publishing multiple-language editions, Rizzoli still enables artful original books with a strong American point of view. They're still making it possible for a community-minded author to dream big and then make it happen.   —R.O.

First published in the United States of America in 2012
by Rizzoli International Publications, Inc.
300 Park Avenue South
New York, NY 10010
www.rizzoliusa.com

© 2012 Richard Olsen

p. 3: Courtesy George Brook-Kothlow; pp. 4, 38 (right top and bottom), 39 (top left), 141 (right): © 2012 Nello di Salvo Archive/Courtesy Paolo Costanzi; pp. 6, 18 (right): Courtesy Bob Nash; p. 14 (top): Courtesy Annie Weedon; p. 14 (bottom left and right), 15 (bottom), 53 (top left): © 2012 Sterling Doughty; pp. 15 (top), 62 (left): Courtesy Emile Norman Charitable Trust; p. 16 (right): Phil Malten/Courtesy George Brook-Kothlow; p. 16 (bottom): Courtesy Goph Albitz; pp. 16 (top left), 26 (top), 28, 31 (left), 35 (right), 38 (left), 39 (middle left and bottom left), 47 (bottom left), 59 (bottom), 97, 101, 147, 148, 150, 151, 152, 153, 155, 173, 174, 175, 176, 177: © 2012 Richard Olsen; p. 18 (top and left), 105 (right): Courtesy Jonathan Kasparian; pp. 19, 63, 65, 66, 68, 69, 98, 103, 104, 106, 107, 108, 132 (bottom left), 186 (left), 189, 190, 192, 193, 194, 195, 196, 197: © 2012 Lucy Goodhart; pp. 20, 21, 22: Peter Stackpole/Courtesy Deva Rajan; p. 23 (bottom left): Courtesy John Peden/The Peden Studio; p. 24 (bottom right): Jay Mrozek/Courtesy Daniel Liebermann; p. 25: Courtesy Daniel Liebermann; p. 26 (bottom): Katrien Vermeire/Courtesy Henry Jacobs; p. 27 (left): Courtesy Sim van der Ryn; p. 30 (top and left middle), 32, 33: Courtesy Barry Downs; p. 30 (middle, right middle, bottom): Courtesy Henry Yorke Mann; p. 31 (right): Courtesy Zoltan Kiss; pp. 34, 46 (left), 50: © 2012 Alexander Vertikoff; p. 36: Courtesy Christopher Day; p. 39 (top right, bottom right and bottom middle): Courtesy Allan Linnemann; p. 40 (left): Pedro Albornoz/Archivo Fundación César Manrique/Courtesy Fernando Ruiz; p. 40 (right): Archivo Fundación César Manrique/Courtesy Fernando Ruiz; p. 41: © 2012 John Witzig; p. 43: Courtesy James Hubbell; pp. 45, 47 (top and bottom right): © 2012 Radek Kurzaj; p. 46 (top right): Courtesy the Bohemian Club; p. 46 (bottom right): from The Simple Home; p. 49: © 2012 J. Claude Mora Fribourg/CH; p. 51: © 2012 Thomas Namey/Namey Design Studios; p. 53 (top right and bottom): Courtesy Sylvia Trotter-Anderson; p. 55: © 2012 The Hedrich Blessing Archive/Chicago Historical Society; p. 56: © 2012 Batista Moon Studios; p. 57: Courtesy Tom Birmingham/Nepenthe restaurant; p. 58 (left): William Turnbull/MLTW Collection (2000–9), Environmental Design Archives, University of California, Berkeley; p. 58 (right top and bottom): Courtesy Obie Bowman; p. 59 (top), 172: Courtesy Michael McNamara; pp. 60 (bottom left), 81 (right): Courtesy Nancy Waite; p. 96 (left): Courtesy Lloyd Kahn; p. 100: Sven Thomasen/Courtesy Cynthia Taylor; p. 111: Courtesy Sheila Smigel; p. 116 (left): Courtesy Mary Breen; pp. 134 (left), 139 (right), 226 (left): Courtesy Sellers & Company; pp. 135, 136, 139 (left): Mark Kaufman/Courtesy Sellers & Company; p. 149 (right): Courtesy Hilary Clark; p. 157: Courtesy Harry H. Gesner; p. 165 (right): Courtesy Tamae Agnoli; p. 171: Courtesy Margaux Kirsch; p. 207 (right): Courtesy Loxi Struckus Hagthrop. All other photographs © 2012 Kodiak Greenwood.

1972

United Nations Environment Programme founded

1970

U.S. Senator Gaylord Nelson organizes first official Earth Day celebration

1972

U.S. Water Pollution Control Act passed

1980

U.S. Comprehensive Environmental Response, Compensation, and Liability Act passed

1972

DDT banned in U.S.

1973

U.S. Endangered Species Act passed

1971

Greenpeace Foundation established

1980

EarthFirst! advocacy group founded

1972

United Nations Conference on the Human Environment

1970

U.S. Clean Air Act passed